IT'S NOT ABOUT THE BEARD

Published by The Big Ideas Library 2015
Copyright © Tom Fitzsimons, 2015

Tom Fitzsimons has asserted his right to be identified as the author of this work.

First published in the United Kingdom in 2015
by The Big Ideas Library

The Big Ideas Library
20 Fountayne Street, York YO31 8HL

A CIP catalogue record for this book is available from the British Library.

ISBN 978-0-9929859-7-4

Typeset by Ned Hoste
Edited by Jacky Fitt
Printed in by CPI Group (UK)

The Big Ideas Library is the publishing division of The Big Ideas Collective Ltd.

IT'S NOT ABOUT THE BEARD

TOM FITZSIMONS

big
ideas
library®

Dedication

"Behind every great work we can find the self-sacrificing devotion of a woman."[1]

To my beautiful partner Zoë, you are my guiding light, my rock, my lover and my friend. Together we will change the world.

"Our victory over addiction will be the laughter of our children."[2]

To my beautiful children, Mason, Niall, Orla and Oliver, thank you for giving up your father for four months to help others. Your love and support make me so proud as a father.

"Sobriety without action is pointless."[3]

To all people struggling with addiction, remember that not only is recovery possible, it is worth it, you are worth it. Take action against your illness and learn to love yourself and above all strive for happiness.

---

1. A dedication on the Brooklyn Bridge to Emily Warren Roebling, wife of bridge builder Washington Roebling whose ill health saw Emily take on and finish the bridge's construction.

2. Tom Fitzsimons

3. Charlie Engle, ultramarathon runner

West Coast

May 20th California

May 29th Nevada

June 11th Utah

June 24th Colorado

July 11th Nebraska

July 11th Kansas

July 24th Missouri

July 30th Illinois

August 5th Indiana

August 12th Ohio

August 16th West Virginia

August 16th Pennsylvania

August 25th New Jersey

August 27th
Coney Island, NYC

East Coast

Contents

Introduction

Writing a book, what could be easier? I seriously thought that when I sat down and started to write about why and how I ran across America in 100 days. What I didn't realise was that writing this book would be more difficult than running itself.

My reading ability has become that poor over the years, so much so that I seldom actually read anything. In fact, I didn't read this book until the editing process. Despite this, however, I feel I probably benefited from not being influenced by anyone else's work, and, had I been comparing my work with another adventurer or author, I've no doubt this book would have remained in my already overcrowded mind.

Being able to re-live my time on the road was everything I wanted it to be and a little more. Before I set off on the run a friend recommended that I took time to enjoy the sights and sounds. This was of course a once in a lifetime opportunity, but sadly I did not listen. *Of course* I did not listen; that's not what adventurers do. We do not listen to anyone but ourselves. If we did we'd have no adventures, as someone will always try and talk you out of a life less ordinary. Yet, this bit of advice was very sound in hindsight. Taking time to enjoy the sights and sounds was something I wished I had done more of, so, no one was going to accuse me of rushing the writing process. It was an opportunity to look at every picture and watch every video diary. It was a time for me to recall conversations I'd had with the people I'd met on the road. It was a time for me to reflect on what I have achieved.

There is so much more to running across America than the actual legwork. In fact if you are intending to read this as a running journal you may be disappointed. If, however, you are interested in a journey of addiction, struggle, laughter, pain, misery, hope, joy, despair and love there's something here for you.

It is not a story of a beard.

At first my magnificent beard was a bit of fun.

I grew it, initially, in homage to Hollywood's fabled runner Forrest Gump. After the first month pounding the roads of the US I was about to shave it off when my brother Sean became quite insistent that I was in fact the biblical character Samson and that my strength was quite clearly coming from my beard. Runners are quite superstitious and therefore I actually believed him and kept the beard. As time went on my beard served a purpose by allowing me to create an alter ego called… wait for it… Mountain Man. Mountain Man would not quit; Mountain Man would not get scared at the trucks and cars speeding towards him; Mountain Man could cope with the crippling pain in his muscles and the isolation of the lonely, empty roads; Mountain Man was a hero. The longer the beard grew, the stronger Mountain Man became.

As soon as the run finished the beard should have come off. Tom Fitzsimons should have returned. Sadly, the beard stayed, my alter ego became my nemesis and nearly destroyed me. When recounting my tales of the run, people would be looking at my beard. When I talked of running over the Sierra Nevada they would ask: "Do you condition your beard?" When I spoke of my continuing battle with alcoholism they would ask: "Who cuts your beard?"

It's not about the beard.

I hope you enjoy reading about my journey as much as I have enjoyed the process of writing about it. It has been emotional.

Live the Life

Tom

CHAPTER 1
April 1988

On the 25th April 1988, I was by awoken by a family friend. Dad was dead.

Though my friend's words were clear, I couldn't get my head around them; I had only been with dad the night before, doing things a father and son do: talking, arguing – finding it hard to show our deep, unshakeable bond.

Dad had died suddenly in the night and, by the time I was awake, his body had been moved by the ambulance team. Perhaps it was because I hadn't seen his body that I hoped he was still alive, that it wasn't happening... that it wasn't real.

It took about two weeks to arrange to fly dad's body back to Belfast – his boyhood home and the city I too had grown up in, a city brimming over with emotional significance. Arriving before him, I had been waiting for his coffin for days, there had been a mix up at the airport and that had meant more delays. During this time I convinced myself that it was all a dream and that my dad would appear and shout, "What about ya!" Hope is a wonderful thing to hold on to. If you have hope you feel you can cope. That hope was finally extinguished when his coffin finally arrived.

The house was packed with people who all went quiet as the hearse pulled up outside. Though I had been through this macabre circus before at my grandfather's funeral, I sensed this was something different. This was the body of a young man. My father was thirty-nine years old when he died, the father of five young children, a dear husband, a brother and a son. This was not a man who died having lived a full life; this was a man who had been taken too young. The knowledge of so many wasted possibilities hung in the air; the atmosphere was heavy with tragedy.

Amongst the Irish Catholic community it is the custom to keep the coffin open for mourners to pay their respects and I had managed to convince myself that I could handle seeing the corpse. I had seen my grandfather's body only four months earlier and took it in my stride. As the eldest male child my job was to stand up and be a man. A man? I was 13 years old. I had only just started listening to music and noticing that I was attracted to girls. My first love was still football and I still enjoyed an ice cream with my mates and playing out till the sun went down.

Too soon, the undertaker lifted the coffin lid and I began to shake.

"No, this can't be! This can't be! This can't be!" I screamed – a boy stunned by the reality of loss and death and unable to cope with the emotional punch of the sight in front of him. My father's bloated face and lifeless hands were all wrong. Dad was an expressive man – so full of physicality and passion. He would always be writing or playing imaginary guitar and reacting to some minor outrage or fit of enthusiasm by throwing his hands in the air. I always remember them being warm and gentle when he gave me a hug, but also firm when I'd overstepped the mark. As the mourners began to cry, I began shouting, "I've got to get out of here! I've got to get out of here!"

I don't remember where I ran or for how long. I just ran and ran until I couldn't run any more, got my breath and ran again. My vision was blurred by my tears and I often stumbled, but running seemed to be the natural thing to do. Running put distance between the truth of the matter and the hope I wanted to cling on to. Yet, the running had to end and soon I found myself again surrounded by the puzzled looks of my family, unable to understand their own grief, never mind mine.

Nobody understood my need to run, but it had helped, briefly, to dull the memories of my father's dead face. When I stopped, the pain came back. Of course, the tragedy of these things is that when so many people are touched, they become self-centred mourners. Each getting through it the only way they can, nobody noticing another's private trauma. Nobody noticed that my world had shattered.

The pain I felt after my father's death created the perfect environment for me to develop a liking for alcohol. The first time I got drunk was on a football trip to Germany. I had gone there about a month after my dad had died. I remember waking up the next day thinking, "Wow I didn't talk about dad once last night." It, alcohol, was to be my saviour, my new love and my confidante.

Quite quickly my drinking developed into a regular pattern. I began working on a building site and had plenty of disposable income. We are not talking paper round pocket money; at the age of 15 I was earning one hundred pounds a week. I was and always have been a hard worker. Working on a building site for most kids would have been a daunting place to be but for me I felt at home. Surrounded by my countrymen they looked after me. Mind you, their idea of looking after me was different to my parents' idea of how I should be brought up. I was influenced by the stereotype of the Irish. I actually believed it! We worked hard and we drank a lot. Looking back I find that quite sad. The Irish, as a nation, have a lot more to offer, unfortunately, the other guys lived up to stereotype. So, from the age of 15 I would be working a 10-hour shift and then hitting the pub for eight pints of lager.

Obviously, this began to impact on my schooling but I had lost interest in being a child and going to school. That opportunity felt like it had been snatched away from me when my dad died. I didn't want to learn how to speak French or how to dissect a frog or read Shakespeare. It had no relevance to my life. I wanted to be a man, I wanted to be something I was too young to be, I wanted to feel alive, I wanted to escape the pain. Alcohol did all of this for me. It made me feel part of the workforce, it made me feel alive with confidence and it made me forget, for a little while anyway.

My drinking got me into trouble very quickly. My first night out in a Wakefield nightclub ended up in a bar brawl, which I was heavily involved in. Here I was, after only drinking for two years, fighting with grown men in a nightclub. Thrown out of the club, the fight spilled onto the street. I found myself attacking another man and punching him to the floor before raining kicks and punches into him. I had become an animal. I had become a criminal. I ran off laughing. These types of incidents were to become a regular occurrence over the next few years.

I often think about environment and culture. Back then I found Wakefield to be a perfect breeding ground for alcohol abuse. We had 'Ten pence a pint night' for a start! There was also a culture of 'this is what we do in Wakefield, we drink...'. One of the things Wakefield is famous for is the Westgate Run – it was seen as a challenge or even a birthright to try to have a drink in every pub on the long stretch of road (that's around 20 bars), to prove your 'worth' as a drinker. This challenge became the norm for me from Thursday until Sunday. I could afford it even at 15.

My relationships with people close to me were becoming strained. My anger was a real issue and I would often take it out on those closest to me. My girlfriend at the time bore the brunt of my fury, both verbally and physically. I think this is important to admit to, as so many people deny it happens. We were in the same nightclub one Saturday evening when I spotted her dancing with another man, something she was more than entitled to do. I saw red and ran onto the dance floor. I took a swing at the man and turning on my ex, kicked her across the dance floor. I felt genuine betrayal and the type of hate that would make a person kill. My head had gone completely. In just six years I had gone from being a normal 13-year-old boy to a violent, abusive drunk.

I needed to get out of the club quickly. I had left my car at my mate's house, so I got in a cab to go back there to sleep. When I got back I started to go over what had happened in my head. The anger surfaced again, building in waves – I was going to sort this out, I couldn't sleep until I had confronted my ex. I got in my car, which I'd owned for just a couple of months. It was a metallic blue Vauxhall Nova SR, not bad for a 19-year-old. It was a great car. It was also super-fast. I drove into Wakefield at high speed, tearing through the rain-soaked January streets. As I got to the town centre I picked up speed, about 80 mph in a 30 mph zone. I had been drinking all day and at that speed I could hardly see out of the window with the rain lashing down. Suddenly, I felt the car slide, it hit a kerb and bounced me into a traffic island, which then sent me hurtling straight towards a shop front.

At 80 mph I was happy, I would put my foot down on the accelerator and go as fast as I could and end it all – that would teach her a lesson, it would also get me away from my crap life. I ended up inside the shop front having crashed through the front security shutters and the main doors. Nothing broken, not even a scratch.

Having caused twenty thousand pounds worth of damage and given a positive breath test I was banned from driving for 16 months and given a 12-month probation order, which involved an alcohol awareness course. This was going to be a changing point in my drinking. Banning me from driving did no good at all. I now had no reason NOT to drink. Someone else could do the driving, while I could get better at drinking.

Chapter 2

27th August 2007

The next 10 years were full of total denial that there was anything wrong with me. Despite several arrests for drunken behaviour, only the people closest to me knew the severity of my drinking. My work suffered because all I wanted to do was get to the pub. I would often have rows with work colleagues, simply so I could storm out of the office and go and get drunk. Unlike the stereotypical alcoholic Irishman, I wasn't living on the street or constantly in and out of jail. I had a management position in a large construction firm. I was in charge of about 40 men, had a company car and a good salary. Yet, I was not happy. All my money was being spent in the pub. Even after the birth of my eldest sons Mason and Niall (Mason was born in February 1997 and Niall in October 1998) and the sadly short-lived relationships with their mothers, I couldn't control the urge to drink. If anything, when the kids came along it got worse. I became very selfish with my time and my money. Holidays were non-existent, as they would use up too much of my drinking money. Living with me must have been a nightmare. The constant fear of whether I was coming home drunk and in a bad mood must have been very frightening but something, at the time, I felt powerless to change.

My decision to quit alcohol was one of the hardest I have ever had to make. Some people will find that hard to understand. How can it be a difficult decision to give up something that was destroying my life? You see, at the time, I didn't realise that alcohol was destroying my life. I had never experienced life without alcohol, so I had nothing to compare it with. In my head the only difference would be that my life would still be as shit, only I would be sober. Alcohol gave me a sense of purpose. My whole day was geared around getting my first drink. Plotting, planning, lying and even stealing to get to the pub. My work, my family, everything was always secondary to getting drunk.

So, how do you give up the one thing that helps you cope? The one thing that you get out of bed for, the one thing you work for. It's not easy is it? We have all tried to give things up for a New Year's resolution and failed after three weeks. Most of the things we give up are pointless – sweets, chocolates, coffee, etc. Why do we fail so miserably? Because it takes will-power, it takes personal sacrifice and none of us likes personal sacrifice and, most importantly, you feel life is boring when you give up. You feel completely worthless. At least when I was drinking I had a social life; I had rows with people, I had laughs with people; if I gave up alcohol I thought I would lose all that.

People still see alcoholism as a sign of weakness rather than an illness. They see it as a failure of self-control. People say, "It's your choice when you drink and how much." That may have been the case when I took my first drink of alcohol but that was when that deal fell apart. More and more evidence is coming to light that alcoholism is an illness, and not just a mental illness but a genetic illness, in other words it's 'hardwired' in our brains before we take our first drink; some may well be predisposed to alcoholic addiction. I certainly don't have any other addictions.

With people continually telling you that alcoholism is not an illness, it is simply a lifestyle choice, it becomes harder still to talk about and makes it difficult to get the right help. How can you get help from your doctor for an illness when the doctor could be doubtful of the severity or cause of your problem?

In May 2001 on a stag week in the Canary Islands I met someone who was to help me make a change, who has and still is, having a profound effect on my life...

Zoë was on the island with her friend Claire. We met in a bar (where else?) and I knew that we had a connection straight away. I am not going to say it was love at first sight but I definitely felt something.

It wasn't going to work on paper – she lived in London and I was in Yorkshire. She had a great, stable life and I was a bit of a wild man. I had two children with two different women and, despite my failings as a partner to their mothers, I made up for it by ensuring I spent almost every weekend with the boys. As you can imagine I wasn't exactly a great 'catch'. Zoë seemed to take it in her stride. She accepted (to her undying credit) that, if she were to have a relationship with me she would also be taking on two children, at least at the weekends anyway.

Our relationship got serious very quickly and by September 2001 Zoë and I moved in together in a small house in Beverley, East Yorkshire. Still working in London through the week, which allowed me my much-loved freedom Monday to Friday, Zoë joined me and the boys on a weekend. It was only when she finished her contract and moved up to Yorkshire permanently that she discovered the extent of my drinking. Still she stayed; thankfully she saw something worth sticking around for.

By June of 2004 I had started a new job with a utility firm. Basically, I had been head-hunted for a position that was going to be a great move for me. The promise of a bigger salary meant that I could drink more, so that was very appealing and I jumped at the opportunity. Quickly I realised I had made a huge mistake. I hated the people I was working with, the location and the work I was doing. It was not the right place for me. After two months of going through the motions my drinking had reached a critical stage, mainly through boredom. My mood was very low and one morning, after a heavy night's drinking, I literally couldn't raise my head off the pillow. I was emotionally and physically wrecked. My body had quit on me. My only thought that morning was that I wanted to die. I wanted to leave it all behind.

I lay in bed emotionless, hoping that I could just sleep it off. After a week in this state Zoë managed to convince me to go and see a doctor.

I arrived at the surgery full of hope; I was going to get the help everyone had been going on about for years. I was about to start a new chapter in my life. I would be sober in a couple of weeks and have a plan of action in place within a month. My mood would lift, the depression would go, I would be able to return to work and most of all, Zoë, and my kids would love me again and trust that I was going to be a human being that was worthy of knowing. The reality was somewhat different ...

I walked into the surgery to be met by a locum doctor who did not look any older than 25. How would this guy understand anything about what I was about to tell him? He had no life skills or experience. Alcoholism is something he would have come across in the student union bar rather than in a clinical situation. I announce that I was an alcoholic, something I had never admitted to myself let alone a doctor. The response was priceless. He looked at me with a vacant stare and said, "Well Tom, you know you have to stop drinking." All that training at medical school for that?

"I know that doctor, that's why I'm here, I need your help."

"No Tom, it's down to you to stop drinking ..." My God, I'm glad I didn't go in with cancer, I would hate to have tackled that on my own. He then gave me a number for the charity Turning Point and wished me well.

Clinging to my disappearing resolve, I went straight from the surgery to Turning Point, I did not feel the same elation I had felt going to the doctor's, I was now worried about the response I would get. Who would understand my problem? Who would listen? The lady I spoke to was great, she seemed understanding and listened to my situation. She didn't judge me or offer advice, she just listened. This was going to work. I was finally going to get help! Then she said the words that would set me back a further 18 months, "We will be in touch." I felt like I had had my heart ripped out. "This is a long process Tom and you will have to wait to see a project worker." This was not going to work. I was not going to get the help I so desperately needed. To wait a few weeks for treatment is not unusual I know, but with addiction, once you have made the decision to get help you are at your lowest point and you need that help immediately. Had I been told to come back on a daily basis I would have done so, but to be told, "We'll be in touch..." knocked the stuffing out of me.

Deflated, I left the charity and went next door to the church. No help there! The priest had watched me come in but made it quite clear he didn't have time to talk. I cried and cried and cried. Sadly, at this point I lost my desire to quit drinking. Clearly, I was a lost cause; I was wasting people's time, I was not worth it. I went back to the pub and had a drink. God it tasted good. There was no waiting list for this, it was a world I knew; I knew the pitfalls, the highs, the lows and the consequences but it was where I felt safe. No one could accuse me of not trying. I had looked for help and there was none. I had put my hands up and admitted my problem – at least in the pub people would listen.

I lost my job. Having only been with a new firm for a couple of months they were perfectly within their rights to tear up my contract. After all, who would knowingly employ an alcoholic? To be fair my boss Noel did look after me financially and paid up the duration of my contract.

So what next? Surely I would struggle to get another job? No, not a problem. Despite me being a bloody liability I was still pretty good at my job. An opportunity came up to work in Northern Ireland, which would mean being away from home all week. The money was good and I figured at least I wouldn't be hurting my family if I went away to drink... I mean work.

I am sure there were times over the years when she regretted staying but Zoë never showed it. She only showed an unconditional love for me that I did not deserve. In September 2004 we had our first child together, my beautiful daughter Orla, quickly followed by my third son Oliver in January 2006. To the outside world everything was great but the cracks were starting to appear and by March 2006 my drinking had reached, quite possibly, its worst point.

Now with two little ones, Zoë had her hands full. I hated being around the house with kids crying and Zoë stressed, I couldn't cope. Mentally I was in a very poor way, I was struggling to keep my alcohol problem from another new employer and my relationship with people around me was at an all-time low. Socially, there was always someone complaining about me to the landlord or the club committee about my abusive behaviour or my drink driving. I just laughed it off and said that when they spent as much as me at the bar then they could complain. Justifying my behaviour by how much money I was spending should have been an eye-opener to how bad things had become.

The Monday after St Patrick's Day Zoë had had enough. I had been drunk for the entire weekend, I had been extremely abusive and looked as though I was on my last legs. She never actually said she was going to leave but things were tense. I had upset and annoyed her in the past but I could see in her eyes that she was beaten and tired of fighting. They say that 'behind every great man is an even greater woman'. Well, behind only the luckiest alcoholics there is a strong and loyal partner – always seeing the best in the person they love and defending their every action. Zoë knew my problems but only on occasion would she get angry about it. What good is getting angry about an illness? She honestly believed that I would beat it and that my true personality would come through. She hoped.

But, this time it was different; Zoë knew that every time I got close to being at rock bottom she pulled me through. She had realised that in order for me to know how much this was hurting her, I had to feel the hurt for myself. The threat of losing Orla and Oliver was quite real on this occasion. Zoë had the opportunity to move back to her folks in Bristol. This would really hurt me. Bristol was a 300-mile round trip from Beverley, so it was out of the question that I could travel every weekend to see the kids. I had been through this before with Mason and Niall and I was terrified it was about to happen all over again. I knew I was about to lose the one person who, through everything, had remained loyal and who loved me unconditionally. Something fell into place that day.

By chance, I received an email from a magazine called *Men's Fitness*. It was about a duathlon. A duathlon is a three-staged event much like a triathlon but instead of the swim/ bike/run set-up it is a run/bike/run. Race distances vary and this race was a 5km run, a 20km cycle and a 2.5km run to be held in September at Windsor. My first reaction was to delete the message, as exercise was something I avoided like the plague. But, for some reason I read a little more and noticed that there was an event for beginners.

Inexplicably, I was drawn to it. My mind started working overtime – was this a sign of what I was supposed to do? I was so desperate to show Zoë I could change that I called her into the room and struck a deal with her there and then: I would train for the race if she would put up with me for a couple more months. She looked at me with amazement. I suppose she could see in my eyes what I had seen in hers – that something was different. She could see that I was serious.

There was of course a little matter of me stopping drinking. Obviously I could not start training whilst I was still drinking. 'Cold turkey' for me? Could I do it? Having drunk enough to 'float the navy' over the weekend, I was probably still pissed when I agreed to the race. So the first day without booze was a little easier than normal, as there was still alcohol in my system. This got me through the day at work, all I had to do was to get past the pub on the way home and I was starting a new life.

Easier said than done. The pub had become my second home – my sanctuary after a hard day. Finding strength from somewhere, but all the time doubting my resolve, I drove a different way home. A small victory perhaps, but it was a turning point, nevertheless. The next test that day was the usual call from the lads asking if I was going to be in the pub; never one to miss a drinking session, if I had received such a call I would have found it impossible to say no. "You could just go in for one," was my default thought. This was never the reality. Even when I only had enough money for one drink it was never enough. I would often attach myself to a group of people in the hope that they would buy me a drink. I switched off my phone.

I managed to get home and felt unusually calm. This was it! Simple! I had cracked it. I had successfully climbed the first hurdle. I had broken the cycle of work, pub, work, pub ... Zoë looked at me to gauge whether I had been drinking. I don't think she could believe that I was actually sober after a day at work. I went upstairs and got my shorts and t-shirt on. "Here goes," I thought, "how hard can it be?"

Beginning to run I remember feeling quite proud of myself for about the first 100 metres, but then reality set in and my pace slowed. This wasn't fun; this was torture. I had made a mistake. Running was not the answer!

Running until you make yourself sick was something you would hear boxers or top sportsmen doing: pushing their bodies to the limit, until breaking point. For them, this was simply the rough with the smooth of training, but for me, I thought I was about to die. Seriously, I thought I was dying. Every footfall on the hard pavement made me feel closer to death. I was shaking and violently sick by the roadside. My heart felt as though it was about to pop out of my chest and my head was throbbing. This was it for sure – I was taking my last breath. What I also felt was shame. I was a fat horrible mess who couldn't run. I was a bloody horrible drunk who was fit for nothing. "As soon as I finish I am going straight to the pub!" I thought. Though I had only run half a mile of my familiar neighbourhood streets I was in a terrible state. Still, when I finished I didn't go to the pub. Not just because I thought I was dying or because I couldn't get off the bathroom floor, but because I felt something else, something that I wanted more of. It was the feeling I came to understand as happiness.

I hadn't been happy for almost 20 years. I'd had moments of laughter and of relief but not true happiness. Even at the birth of my children – there was too much anxiety and excitement to just feel happy. The ideal of pure happiness, for me, is when you forget everything for a moment and your mind is still and it is just about you and a feeling of inner peace within your own mind. You are happy with 'you'. Now that might seem a little selfish, but I truly believe that this is the key to my recovery. I needed to be happy with me. I needed to forget what others thought and concentrate on me. The man I believed I was. I needed to even forget about my family troubles...work...money...the past and concentrate on making myself better. Drink was my problem. This was, and still is, about me.

From that painful first run, a new me was born and my life changed beyond recognition. I began to lose the weight I had gained during my heavy drinking. I had topped the scales at 18.5 stones with a 44-inch waist but after about a year of training, I had managed to get down to 13 stones. It wasn't easy. But the feeling of happiness that came from the run – that euphoria mixed with satisfaction and pride – made me do it and stick to it. No fleeting feeling of drunken relief could match this new high.

There was a lot of pain, but soon I was running almost every day and I upped the stakes by running in some competitive races. I then reached the stage where I was comfortably running 10 kilometres and was starting to tackle half marathons. Had anyone told me earlier that this would be me I would have laughed. I never believed this was something I could have ever achieved. Yet, I managed to complete the Newark Half Marathon in August 2006 just five months after starting running.

Achievements like this seem trivial – everyone knows a runner; however, these milestones were crucial markers on my road to recovery. Without marking your achievement you can never move forward. When you are drunk you never move forward; you are always moving in either reverse or not at all. Your life goes nowhere and you can never see that changing. By running 10 kilometres you can then make a plan to go further or faster and you can chart your progress. It gives you direction and stops the endless drifting.

Running also allows you time to think without interruptions. Having spent so much time in the pub I never allowed myself time to think or make decisions for myself. There was always someone offering their opinion or, more often, their misguided advice. When I was running I would often go over things in my head and would sometimes forget that I was running at all. Where had things gone wrong? How could I have hurt people I loved so much? How I was going to change even more? How was I going to redeem myself and make things right with my family? I had a lot of running to do.

I had cracked it. I had done what every other alcoholic had failed to do. I was able to control my drinking with running. It was that simple, none of this nonsense they tell you in Alcoholics Anonymous. "You have to stay sober for the rest of your life..." not me, not Tom Fitzsimons, I was better than everyone else. All I had to do was run.

I decided that I had 'earned a pint' and quickly developed a 'pint per mile' reward system. Run six mile, drink six pints; run eight miles, drink eight pints. Half marathon – happy days! This continued for months and, despite completing my first full marathon in Belfast in 2007, I was once again losing control of my life. My 'pint per mile' method had been long forgotten, as once more I used every excuse I could to drink rather than run – I was injured or maybe I was having a rest day. By June 2007 I really felt I had had enough but it wasn't until my final drinking session on August 27th 2007 that I finally managed to take my finger off the self-destruct button.

I had been away on an annual rugby trip that used to be everything I loved: lads away, good food and plenty of drinking. This year I'd had a short period of sobriety before the trip and told the lads I would not be drinking. At first this was met with the usual, "What a load of bollocks Tom!" but the lads had seen how much I had achieved over the previous year and were pretty impressed. As well as running a marathon I had also managed to lose almost four stones in weight. They, like me, wanted to believe I could do this. And I did, almost... We met at the cricket club on the Friday morning as usual and, as the men got started on their beer and lagers, I had a coffee. It felt a little strange but I was determined to stick with the plan. Everything went well until Sunday afternoon. We always stopped in a town called Ashby-de-la-Zouch for the last drinking session of the trip. I always loved this session and as I saw my mates getting stuck into their pints of Guinness I pushed my latte aside. "Pint of Guinness please, love." There was an uneasy silence as the barmaid passed over the brimming glass. My audience looked on as in two gulps the velvety cold black liquid disappeared. "Another pint please, love." That too disappeared within a heart beat. "Another pint please and a whiskey." The uneasy silence was broken by a shout, "For fuck's sake, he's back!" loud cheers and laughter filled the air. I was too busy to notice. Eight pints in forty-five minutes and four double whiskeys later... well, I do not remember much else of the day.

When I woke on Monday morning, August 27th, I knew that was it. I had finished for good. After all these years I just knew that day was it. My whole attitude had changed. I felt terrible about letting Zoë and the children down and for the first time in a long, long time I felt thoroughly ashamed. Oddly, not by my drinking but my loss of control. I was embarrassed by my lack of conviction.

My attitude toward my recovery also changed on that day. August 27th 2007 will remain my most special of days. It's the date I mark as my sobriety day – the change I craved, the focus I needed, I now knew I had found within myself.

Thinking about change is one thing and I found this quite helpful in the early days, but I would often be going over so much in my head that nothing ever seemed to be resolved. So, I took to writing things down as soon as I got back from a run. Actually writing it down acted like a contract for me. A contract between me and sobriety. If I wrote it down I would inevitably act on it. Also, if I spoke about it or told someone what I was thinking then I would always do my best to do it. This was to prove I was serious about making amends.

One of my ideas was to try to help others. It occurred to me that as I wasn't a natural athlete, if I could do it, anyone could. I therefore set about finding out how I could become a personal trainer. Incredible! Me, the once eighteen stone alcoholic, a personal trainer! But I wanted to pass on my experience to others. In my mind, I was the ideal candidate for the job – a real-life example of change. I wanted to inspire change in others, too. So, at the end of 2007 I started to train as a personal trainer and in May 2008 I finally received my qualifications. This has enabled me to pass on my knowledge to so many people, some of whom have also had issues with alcohol.

Another idea was to try, one day, to run a marathon. Again, looking back it is amazing to think that, to date, I have now completed over 20 marathons and ultra-marathons. Ultra-marathons opened up a whole new world for me. I never even knew these races existed. Running the traditional 26.2-mile marathon seemed crazy enough in the early days. I had heard about these mad blokes who ran further, some as much as 100 miles in a single effort. This blew my mind to know that some people were able to push their bodies this far. I was so intrigued I decided to give it a go. The distances vary from 30 miles and back-to-back 45-mile events. The whole process seemed fantastic. My personal highlight was completing the Marathon des Sables in April 2010.

The Marathon des Sables is a 155-mile race through the Sahara Desert. Daytime temperatures reach 50 degrees and we had to carry our own food and equipment to last the week – that's an 11kg backpack! Day four was the longest and most gruelling stage; at 55 miles, it took me almost 21 hours to complete. When I crossed the finish line I was asked how I felt and I replied instantly that I was proud to be a human being and I hadn't felt like that for a long time. The emotion of recovering from alcoholism and being able to achieve that level of fitness and commitment was immense for me and I cried for two hours solid whilst watching the sun come up over the desert.

Today, as my recovery continues, I know I will always face a daily battle with temptation, but things are easier now and I am committed to changing people's perception of my illness and of addiction in general. Back to 2009, and whilst listening to a race brief, someone asked us assembled runners: "Why are you doing this?" 'this' being a 45-mile cross-country run. The race director's reply was immediate and fantastic, and it remains a very special mantra that I live my life by. He simply said:

"You are a focused individual who wants to achieve."

Chapter 3

Moon Landing

You, like me, have probably often listened to the older generation refer to their 'moon landing' moment – a moment in time when they could remember exactly what they were doing when something truly historic happened. So, referring to the first moon landing on 20th July 1969, their moment might have been the Kennedy assassination on November 22nd 1963, the fall of the Berlin Wall in November 1989, or the collapse of the twin towers in September 2001, which I reckon is our most recent 'moon landing' moment. The significance of the event made people stop and think, watch and learn; all of them realising that on that day, at that exact moment, the world changed forever.

I have always wanted a 'moon landing' moment, something that didn't just change the world around me but also changed *my* world.

This finally happened on October 24th 2012 when I heard about the Red Bull Stratos team. Now, I can hear you saying, "Come on Tom, the Red Bull Stratos team is not a moon landing moment!" but remember, I wanted something that changed *my* world. Let me explain...

The team decided that they were going to attempt a parachute jump from the very edge of Earth's atmosphere, basically attempting to set the altitude and speed free-fall record from space.

To reach the height required, the pilot, Felix Baumgartner, would have to travel in a specially designed capsule attached to a weather balloon. The whole thing sounded like something dreamed up by a couple of seven-year-olds in a playground. It was beyond my comprehension as to how and why they would attempt such a thing. Why would anyone want to put themselves in so much danger? That's what makes it a moon landing moment for me. It is beyond normal human thinking! To land on the moon, to kill a president, to fly an airliner into a building. Until you actually see it with your own eyes, you can't comprehend it and in Red Bull's case it seemed impossible, crazy, dangerous, a waste of money! We have been socially conditioned to only accept so much; to live within the norms set by our parents and society – bound by the limits set by others. Yet, these guys were taking seemingly unquantifiable risks. I know there were lots of scientific boffins involved but one mistake and Felix wasn't going to be seeing his family again. It was as simple as that. Despite those great risks Red Bull had faith in the ability of everyone involved to achieve their joint goal.

This is what I call blind faith. Going into something without truly knowing the outcome. All our moon landing moments involve blind faith. The ordinary people who used their bare hands to pull down the Berlin Wall, they had immense faith – they had no idea what the future would hold. Would they be accepted? Could they unite a fractured country? They took the risk. They knocked the wall down anyway, having faith in themselves and those around them being true to their word and fighting for a different, a better future.

Isn't this what also captures our attention? Not knowing what will happen, that excites us.

The beauty of a moon landing moment is also that we only see the finale. We don't see the hours of planning and preparation, but I guess that's what also makes them stand out. If you have ever built with Lego you will know what I mean. When you open a box of Lego you are faced with about 1,000 pieces and an instruction book. Again, it's in our nature to go straight to the final page and look at what this pile of brightly coloured plastic bricks is eventually supposed to look like. It's at that moment when most of us look at our kids and say, "I will do it later," put the pieces back in the box and walk away. Eventually, after wide-eyed pleading you relent and start at page one, "Piece of piss this Lego malarkey," you say to yourself before realising there are 99 pages of instructions to go. Slowly working through the booklet you eventually end up with a boat or a spacecraft. Now, because you have built it you don't get that 'wow' factor when it's done. You've seen enough. Leave it on the table and watch your child's face light up when they see it for the first time. That's the wow factor!

Not fully understanding what was about to happen next really added to my moon landing moment ...

I had suggested to Orla and Oliver that we should watch the Red Bull event live, as it was being shown via the Internet. I thought it would be pretty cool for us to join millions of other families across the globe watching this fantastic 'whatever it was' event.

Orla agreed, Oliver wasn't so keen. Turning on a computer without playing games seemed pointless to him. I suppose at six I would have been the same; however, Orla grabbed a chair beside me and we started to watch. The launch had us excited, as, apparently there were so many thing that could go wrong, the commentator insisting that this was a critical point in the whole expedition. Not knowing what to expect, I sat in amazement as Felix and his balloon rose high above the Earth. The images blew my mind. For me going this high in a balloon was more impressive than doing it in a space shuttle. This was beyond all the norms, no safety net, no comfort zone. I know I was definitely out of mine and I was only sitting in front of my computer.

Over the next two hours we watched as the balloon rose higher and higher into the atmosphere. I began to think that Orla would surely lose interest, as it was taking so long. Two hours in the life of an eight-year-old is a long time. She never moved. I think she knew this was going to be special.

Eventually, the capsule reached 128,100 feet above the Earth. I watched as Felix edged towards the lip of the capsule and gasped as I saw the world from a completely different angle. It looked beautiful! "The world is a magnificent place," I heard myself say.

I had never viewed the world as beautiful. I hated the world and all it had given me: childhood poverty, parental addiction and death, violence, racism and, of course, my own alcohol addiction. I had hated the world for as long as I could remember. But, in that moment, looking at what Felix saw I took my phone out and photographed the TV screen. That's how excited I was. I wanted to capture the moment. I wanted to have proof that I was there, watching live.

And then he did it! Felix threw himself out of the capsule and he began to fall.

I held my breath. I had never seen anyone travelling so fast without an engine attached. He started to spin, I feared the worst. How could I explain this to Orla if it went wrong? I could feel her little heart pumping out of her chest. Felix stabilised the spin and continued to fall for what seemed an eternity. He was in free-fall for over four minutes. To fall for over four minutes is beyond crazy. I have never before and probably will never see anyone doing this again. The parachute opened and the cheering started. We could breathe again. Orla was cheering along with me and Zoë. He'd only gone and done it! He had jumped from the edge of space and survived.

As Felix landed in the desert of New Mexico he dropped to his knees and my cheers turned to tears, as the emotion of the last few hours came out. I will never know what Felix felt at that exact moment but I wanted to find out. I wanted my moment where the world was watching. I wanted to achieve my potential.

Within a week I had decided that I was going to run across the USA. Funnily enough, I don't specifically remember the time or place the idea gelled in my mind, or having had a conversation with Zoë, but I am sure if I did she would have given me her usual sigh and, "OK Tom, let's do this!"

As a matter of fact, I'm pretty sure there was no conversation. I am pretty sure I just went ahead and sent an email to a potential sponsor. I knew nothing would happen unless I managed to get the backing of at least one major company. It all hinged on finance. I believe anyone can change the world...if they have the money to get started.

Awaiting a sponsor's reply is usually a long wait. Lots of companies will say, "Do get in touch," responding with, "We'll see what we can do." Most never reply. But, I had a good feeling about this company. I had spoken at their annual conference in Berlin earlier that year. The Managing Director had spoken to me afterwards, he was very supportive of all I had done and commented that if I needed help in any way that I should give him a call.

It was actually at that Berlin conference that the notion of running across the USA entered my brain. During the Q&A at the end of my spot, a lady in the audience asked me what I had planned for the future. Being an international conference in front of a global audience I didn't want to say the Leicester Marathon, not that there is anything wrong with the Leicester Marathon, it's a bloody good race, but I suspect that the audience was expecting a little more. "I'd like to run across the USA." I spoke clearly and confidently, almost convincing myself. It must have been in my grey matter somewhere and I am glad I said it. When you say something like that in front of a large audience it kind of calls your bluff. I've always believed you shouldn't say things you can't back up.

The wait, as I have said, for a sponsor's reply, can be soul destroying. I never liked the whole process of asking for money but since starting my running I found that it was part and parcel of being an adventurer. In fact, the best adventurers tend to be the best at asking for money. I was brought up to work for everything I had but I realised that a project of this scope needed more than I could save in a lifetime.

I sent the email on Saturday and was not expecting to hear back for a few weeks at least. I actually remember sighing when I clicked 'Send', thinking it would never really happen, so what had I got to lose?

Much to my surprise at 8.30 p.m. on Monday evening I received a reply. I was a little apprehensive opening the email, as I presumed it would be a "Thanks but no thanks" message, but instead the initial response seemed very positive. The sponsor asked for a little more information about the run and asked how much help I was looking for. Wow, it wasn't a yes but it sure as hell was not a no. I hadn't even thought of how much support I needed! I hadn't planned much at all and had very little information on what was needed to complete my challenge.

That evening Zoë and I sat down and came up with some pretty crude calculations. I like to keep things simple: flights, accommodation, support vehicle and food. That was it, the four things I needed to complete my journey. I quickly added things up and sent my sponsor the information they required. They responded the very next day to say that they would hope to be in a position to help. That was a yes to me! Having a sponsor was a big boost to my confidence. I was now all systems go to get organising the rest of the details, or as Zoë so eloquently put it, "How the fuck are we going to do this one, Tom?"

The planning of an event is often an afterthought for me. I don't actually like the detail, I like the doing part. I suppose every adventurer has different strengths. Never a methodical organiser, I'm a "Let things develop and see what happens" kind of adventurer.

I decided to go and listen to Mark Beaumont speak at my local theatre in Wakefield. Mark is a Scottish adventurer, most notably cycling around the world in a record time. He has also cycled the length of the Americas and carved out a successful media career. Mark's endeavours are an inspiration to me and I gained a lot from his talk. I was also amazed at the amount of planning that went into his trips. During the Q&A I asked him if all the planning was necessary, as lots of his journeys went awry. He was adamant that he needed the planning in place to feel comfortable and to ensure a project's success but also acknowledged that sometimes flying by the seat of your pants is necessary too. I think he knew having spoken with me during the interval that, rightly or wrongly, I was definitely going to fly by the seat of my pants.

"Rules are for the guidance of wise men and the obedience of fools."

I love this quote, it sums up my thoughts on the rule book. Anyone that knows me will tell you that I don't like rules and regulations. I am not a law-breaker, I fully respect the rule of law but I hate following rules for the sake of it. I feel constrained by other people's limitations.

So, I kept things as basic as I could. Start in San Francisco and run east. There was no other brief. Just run across America. Adding up the figures, however, I realised that having a moon landing moment was going to be expensive, very expensive! It was time to get serious. It was time to start acting like a global adventurer.

Over the next few weeks I tried to keep myself calm. I needed to establish a few things in my own mind. Firstly, could I actually do the run? Was it within my capabilities? That was easily answered as it had been done before. If it's been done before then it is possible. Secondly, when was I going to do it and how long was it going to take me? This proved a little trickier to answer.

To complete the run I had to cover just over three thousand miles. Simple maths told me that 30 miles per day for 100 days would be the target. The other option was a marathon per day. I figured if your only job every day was to run, why would you limit yourself to a marathon? There was at least twelve hours per day available to run. Let's make the most of them. So, 30 miles a day it would be to complete the challenge. As my sobriety date is 27th August I wanted to tie that into the event, figuring that I could either start or finish on that date. Starting in August would expose me to the risk of very bad winter weather. I didn't fancy struggling over the Rockies in a snow storm. So, the decision was made for me really. I would aim to finish the run on the 27th August 2013. That meant that I would have to start on May 20th. It was already early November 2012, which left just seven months to put everything in place.

Now, some people take years planning events like this, but some take so long in the planning that they miss the opportunity to do the event itself. I was not going to miss this opportunity.

I become a little selfish at times like these. At no stage did I ever think of the impact of me being away for so long would have on Zoë and the children. Looking back, they never entered my thought process until Christmas. It's OK saying I will be away for 100 days but with travel either side that equates to nearly four months away from home. Four months that Zoë would be alone without my support and four months that the children would be without their dad. I had mixed emotions about this. I knew that Zoë would be more than capable of coping without me around. In fact I'm sure it is sometimes easier when I'm not around (I am a bit of a nuisance!). My two youngest children have been brought up to know that dad does unusual things. He is and never will be a 'normal' dad. They loved it when I was planning my adventure in the Sahara Desert. Even though they were very young they fully embraced the adventure. This was very different though. I was only away for two weeks during my Sahara trip – this was four months.

Oliver was just about to turn seven. I remember my own father going off to work in London when we lived in Belfast. He worked there for six months and I was left felling very isolated and alone. My mother and sisters seemed to dominate the house and I missed a male role model. I was struggling to think of Oliver feeling the same. How could I justify doing that to my children?

"Be the change you wish to see in the world" Gandhi

I suppose Gandhi's quote was how I justified leaving my partner and children. Zoë has always known since the day I sobered up that I would not be happy until I had helped as many other people in the world as I could who suffered the illness of addiction. Quite early on in my recovery I knew and firmly believed that it was my duty to help those who had not yet discovered this fantastic new world of sobriety. I stood up and decided to practise what I was preaching. I was telling people that they could achieve anything they wanted. I was instilling in my children a belief that greatness was upon them but here I was, two years after my desert run not achieving my own greatness. I needed to *be the change!* Zoë knew this and I think when I told Orla and Oliver my plans they knew it too. I was so proud of my two little babies being so supportive of their dad. Their willingness to sacrifice their time with me to help others is a source of great inspiration to me. They are totally awesome.

My older son Niall doesn't live with me but again when I told him my plans he was totally behind me. He is so laid back about everything but he did show a little concern about my safety. I assured him that every precaution would be taken to make sure I was safe. He trusted me, I'm proud of that.

To be truthful, I did not have time to worry too much about the impact of the trip on my family as I had so much to do. Most importantly I needed to get my knee repaired. When planning this event I had forgotten this minor detail. I had extremely bad knee pain every time I ran. This had started after a race called Hell On The Humber. This night time ultra-race involved running over the Humber Bridge as many times as you could in 12 hours. It was a bloody great race, as I had great company with my good friend George Henderson. We managed 44 miles that night, which we were both pretty pleased with. But, as soon as the running stopped I felt an immense pain in my left knee and I knew it was more sinister than a muscle tear.

CHAPTER 4
Leaving Home

The doctor's first diagnosis was a damaged medial ligament. I was not convinced. He was the doctor though and I was sent for eight weeks physiotherapy. Despite my insistence that the pain was not getting any better they continued to treat my medial ligament. This finally came to a head when after a rather heated discussion with a physiotherapist I put my finger in exactly the place I was getting the pain. "That's a cartilage tear!" she said, "I have been trying to tell you this for weeks!" was my reply. I needed an MRI scan, which meant another trip back to my doctor who could refer me for a scan. The result was as expected. I had a one-centimetre tear in my cartilage and would require surgery. The trouble was we were already in December. I had a three-week wait until I saw the specialist who then informed me it would be a further 16 weeks before surgery. This was not the news you want to hear before running three thousand miles across America.

I was beginning to wonder whether this run was really meant to be. As well as the knee injury and, even though I had secured a big sponsor, I was struggling to raise the rest of the funds. Time was running out. Decisions about whether to proceed or postpone had to be made and fast. Zoë and I struggled with this all over Christmas of 2012. Both of us had a clear vision of what we wanted to achieve and both of us knew I was capable of doing it, we just wanted something to go our way. We wanted confirmation that we were doing the right thing.

On the first Sunday of 2013 we went to church as usual. Life Church in Bradford is a Christian church with so much love and guidance it had allowed me to regain my faith, something I had lost, along with too many other things, at the bottom of a pint glass.

The leadership team announced their vision for 2013 in the form of one word. This word would set the tone of everything that was to be done in the church and in the community over the following year. Zoë and I were quite excited by the build-up. We expected the word to be 'Love' or 'Honesty' or even 'Friendship'. We did not expect 'Outrageous'! Yes, the Life Church word for 2013 was Outrageous. Zoë and I looked at each other and both laughed and cried simultaneously. What could be more outrageous than risking everything and running across the USA? Our journey was blessed by a higher power. We left the church with renewed vigour that all our hard work would pay off, that the newly named **Run4Sobriety** would change lives – God was coming with us.

After several attempts at jumping the queue it was decided that knee surgery would have to wait until after the run. I could have quite easily used the torn cartilage as an excuse but I remembered all the excuses I used to use to avoid sobriety. There are no valid excuses to stay drunk. I wanted people to see this. Nothing should get in the way of being able to live life to its full potential. Nothing would stop me from achieving this goal.

This mindset was the same for the financing of the trip. The main sponsor was secured in writing by March and flights were also generously covered by Kenwood travel, which was a fantastic help. I also decided to do a treadmill marathon challenge in the centre of Wakefield one Saturday afternoon to raise awareness and more funds. I had to borrow a treadmill from a friend and ran for just under five hours whilst my brother Sean and good friend Catherine toured the shopping centre with collecting buckets. Yes guys, we had resorted to begging and, although I managed to raise over £200, it was great but not nearly the amount we needed. I was receiving some personal donations from friends and family, which I will be forever thankful for, but I was still struggling with the shortfall. Again, it could have been an excuse to postpone but instead I decided to go all in. I had a small personal training business that I had built up since 2008. It was a nice second income and had served me well. The gym from which I ran my business was the only asset worth selling, so, after a long discussion with Zoë the decision was made to sell everything and close the business. Anyone thinking this trip was easy for me, think again! Selling my business was singularly the hardest decision I had to make. My business had symbolised how far I had come since gaining my sobriety. To sell it was my ultimate sacrifice. There was no turning back now. The day the equipment went I sat down in my empty gym and cried. It was the one and only time I doubted what I had done. Had I risked too much? Only time would tell.

I always knew that the key to success on this adventure would be the crew. Zoë was always going to be my closest team member. She knew how I worked and the levels of achievement I expect from everyone around me. The sad thing was there was no possible way for her to join me in the States. Zoë was due to return to work in the April of 2013. When she had left her job back in 2004, just before Orla had been born, we took the decision that she would not return to work until the children were settled in school, yet, secretly, I think she was itching to get back into work mode. She had been a fantastic support, helping me launch my personal training and speaking businesses, but there is no substitute for going out into the big bad world and earning your own money. I was quietly happy that she was able to go back to work, although I knew it would be a massive shock to the children, as not only would dad be away for four months but also their mum would be rushing to get to work every morning. I knew that Zoë could cope. Zoë would be the brains of the whole media operation back in the UK. She would also pretty much do everything else ... apart from running of course!

What I needed was a driver. And not just a driver, they had to be a route scout, weather forecaster, accommodation and meal finder, on the ground media wrangler and 24/7 support person. To do this they would also need to be someone who could take four months off work, without pay. Someone who was prepared to drive six miles at a time and then sit waiting for me in the searing desert heat of Nevada (amongst other places) whilst waiting for me to arrive at the agreed checkpoint; someone who was not fussy about sleeping in cheap motels or camping at the side of the road; someone who could put up with my mood swings that ranged from Zen Buddhist to Genghis Khan; someone who believed in me and why I needed to do this. There was only one person that fitted the bill – my brother Sean.

There was only one small problem; apart from a few trips to Amsterdam Sean had never actually left the UK before. Despite being 30 Sean still lived at home with mum and my other brother Adrian. What I was asking would also mean Sean taking on the biggest challenge of his life. It would mean leaving his young son Jude, whom he adored and who worshipped him – Sean might not be perfect but he is a great father. Leaving Jude behind would, in my opinion, be the only stumbling block. We invited Sean to the house to discuss the whole plan. The main selling point of the journey was that Sean would be able to say that he was part of something fantastic. That he would be setting a standard for Jude to follow. It would also be a great way of strengthening our brotherhood bond.

When I was 20 and Sean was 12 we had about a year of being very close. I was playing football at the time for the Ferryboat pub team. This was not Premier League stuff but it was something I loved to do. For that one season Sean came with me to every match to see his big brother play. In fact he even got an award at the end of the season for Supporter of the Year. I wasn't really a great role model. Even at that age Sean had witnessed me at my violent worst and on many occasions was on the receiving end of my drunken rages. I did not deserve his support back then, although I didn't know that at the time. I just thought I was acting like a dad, that I was teaching him how to be a man in a tough world.

In September 1995 I left for Australia and he was the only person I really missed. I never told him that. Of course I didn't, I was a rough tough 20-year-old concrete worker. I didn't show emotion. I don't think I knew how to – I still don't think I know how to! On my return in March 1996 our relationship had changed. While I had been away Sean had grown up a little, he had experienced life without his big brother, he didn't look up to me any more.

Over the few next years, as my drinking became steadily worse, we saw less and less of each other. In fact we would go for months without so much as a phone call. Sadly, our family dynamic is too fractured to talk about in this book – not talking to each other seemed sometimes safest.

Sean and I only really started to connect again when I started my journey of recovery. I think like most people he saw my efforts as a pitiful gesture and that, inevitably, I would return to drinking. After a few years though he, like everyone else, realised that I was serious and our relationship began to slowly change. After the birth of his son he began to ask me for advice on dad stuff. I was honoured. We began to rebuild that brother connection.

His decision to agree to come with me on my journey was crucial to its success. I was putting my faith in him. I personally think that was the one thing that sealed the deal. I had shown faith in him. I knew he could do a great job for me but also the journey would be great for him. I am thankful he almost instantly agreed in principle to coming on this magnificent adventure with me. He would have to get permission from his employer and discuss it with his son's mother, but everything looked good. Sean was part of the team.

During the prep for the run I watched a film called *Running the Sahara*, which charted the progress of Ray Zahab, Charlie Engle and Kevin Lin, as they ran across the Sahara Desert. Apart from being hugely inspirational, the film was also a bit of an eye-opener as to the solitude of such a challenge – not only for the runner but also for the support crew. My 'crew' being just Sean was not going to work. Sean would need a bit of support too.

My nephew Connor was 18 and, I guess, like many 18-year-olds he was a little bit lost. He was struggling to find what direction his life would go. I had an idea that maybe he would fancy a bit of adventure for a month or so. I ran the idea past Sean and he loved it. Sean and Connor have very similar personalities and got on well together, certainly an 18-year-olds point of view would certainly give us a different angle and (no doubt) provide us with some entertainment along the way. Connor is pretty cool and would be great to have on the trip. Zoë, Sean and I agreed to ask him and thankfully he agreed. We would also be joined by Catherine for two weeks after Connor had flown home. A great supporter of the treadmill marathon and the whole trip, I was also really pleased to have Catherine on board; it also meant that Sean had support for the first six weeks of the challenge. My little crew was all set and ready to go.

So there we had it, Zoë at home doing the tough stuff, Sean as driver and lead support crew, Connor as number two support crew (and chief entertainer until Utah) and Catherine, again support crew through Utah and some of Colorado. Few in number and totally lacking experience, but what they lacked in experience they made up in commitment. They would not be paid, they would not be given medals at the finish, they would suffer almost every day but they still committed and with that commitment we could not fail... could we?

The Pledge
Rather than asking people for money to donate to a charity, I decided that I would ask for people to commit to a sobriety pledge. My frustration at the difficulty of raising enough money to actually keep the run a reality led me to this decision; the financial stress was almost too much to bear

at times. I felt pledges were a simple way of people supporting those who have addiction issues.

We set up a simple website to allow people to read more about what we were doing and then pledge their support. This was a free pledge system but I still got lots of grief for it! Within 24 hours I had received a message from someone saying how dare I ask people to stop drinking, after all they didn't have a problem with alcohol... I stayed calm and explained that no one was asking people to stop drinking for good, or to suggest they had a drink problem. It was merely a way for people to show their support for someone who did have a drink problem by staying away from alcohol for a few days. My explanation fell on deaf ears. It was at that moment I realised that for every person who has an adventurous mind or an big idea to help people, there will always be someone who finds fault... Well, sod them!

Happily, the majority of people understood my idea and the pledges came in thick and fast. In the end the total pledges made topped 171,428 and equalled 3,000 days of sobriety, together with 26 lifetime pledges. I also decided to offer a lifetime pledge for those who had already committed to a life without alcohol. For me this was totally fantastic. I do hope that I can do these pledges again.

Leaving Home

I put off writing this section for a long time. I suspect it may be due to the pain it caused Zoë and the children but also how it made me feel.

I was pretty rubbish the last few weeks before leaving for the States. I had become a little distant from everyone, as I knew it was going to be so hard to leave them. It's easier to leave someone when you've had a fight with them, right? My inability to get my frustrations out in an adult manner can become quite destructive. I was very keyed up and became increasingly critical of all of Zoë's efforts and really shut her out completely. She dealt with it brilliantly ... She ignored it!

The week before I left we went to church as a family and also decided to have a lunch out and then a trip to the cinema. The church service lifted my spirits and I held Zoë's hand as the service drew to a close. She always knows that when I hold her hand in public it's got to be a special moment. We then went into the church shop to buy a few things for my journey. I needed a journal to write down my thoughts as I made my way across the continent. I had visions of well-written logs with dates and times written it perfect handwriting. (This was not going to be the case.) I got a beautiful leatherbound journal and wrote a message in the front:

My journal for Run4Sobriety 2013

"May these words inspire future generations to fight against the horrible illness that is addiction.

May these words show my children that their dad was a man of conviction and fight but ultimately goodness.

May these words allow one addict to find sobriety.

May these words be blessed by God."

Tom Fitzsimons, May 2013

Sadly, I rarely wrote in the journal as my handwriting is appalling and I became embarrassed by it. In the end I used video diaries instead to log the journey.

As well as the journal I also bought a new Bible. It had a beautiful zip leather cover and was ideal for travelling. I chose my items and gave them to Zoë to buy as she had also picked up a few bits.

We left church and made our way to the cinema. We decided to see the movie first then to eat later. As we were a little early for the movie we sat in the car park and I decided to look at my new Bible. As I opened the bag a little card fell out. Written on it was my favourite Bible quote *Philippians 4:13*

"I can do all things through Christ who gives me strength."

I pretty much live my life by this quote. Zoë had seen it at the cash register and bought it for me. I was so happy she knew how much it meant to me. My joy was short lived, however, as when I unzipped my beautifully bound Bible I found it was damaged. One page seemed to be torn and irregular. My first reaction was, "I don't believe this. I can't even buy a Bible without it being damaged." I was so upset, I wouldn't be able to change it as I was flying out on the following Wednesday. But, when I looked closer I saw that the corner paper had not been properly cut. It folded over perfectly and as I calmed down I realised I could cope with this minor imperfection. Looking again, I saw the damaged page also held *Philippians 4:13*. I jumped out of the car, as I could not cope with what was happening. After a minute I composed myself, got back in and showed Zoë. It was the first time in all the years I've known her that she has shown genuine shock at the power of God. He truly was with us. We could do all things through Him that gave us strength.

The Bible incident really helped to settle me down. The next few days were nice steady days doing my last minute bit of shopping. Buying £157 worth of sun cream, Vaseline and blister plasters was pretty embarrassing. I also finally had enough money to buy a couple of pairs of trainers. It was pretty cool going into my local Up and Running store telling them my plans. Mind you, I am not sure the guy believed me.

Our final day was pretty hectic. We would be flying from Heathrow early on Wednesday morning, which meant we would all have to stay in a hotel the night before. Sean had already said goodbye to his son Jude so he was pretty cut up all the way down to London. I was thankful to be able to spend one last night with the children. Sadly, Niall could not make the journey with us so we said our goodbyes on the Monday evening. He made it so easy as he just hugged me and told me he loved me.

Orla and Oliver were super cute at dinner that night. Oliver even drew me a picture telling me he loved me, totally unprompted. Orla quickly followed with a beautiful picture with the same message. I admit I didn't sleep much that night. The kids took long time to settle in our hotel room – my mind too was racing and I was kind of glad in a way that we had that early flight the next day. I didn't want to make the day any harder for all of us. After a final round of coffees in the departure lounge

I gave the kids the biggest hug I could, turned to Zoë to see the pride in her face, not a tear, rock solid as ever. I also was pretty solid, as I knew I was coming back, but first I was going to make a better future for us all. In the only way I knew how I was going to make a change for myself and for others. I was going to make them proud of me. I was going to run across America.

CHAPTER 5

Heading East

Sitting in the filtered atmosphere of the Boeing cabin high over the Atlantic, I thought back over my moon landing moment and knew that, to be sat where I was, it was a little more complicated. The reasons for my run across the USA probably began forming as far back as 2010, the year I completed the Marathon des Sables, my biggest challenge since gaining my sobriety in 2007.

I've already touched on this seemingly mad multi-day endurance event, which requires competitors to run 155 miles across the Sahara Desert, over six days, carrying their own supplies... If you can't carry it you can't have it!

Billed as "The toughest footrace on earth", and I can assure you it lives up to its name, I am very proud to say I completed it. I was never going to win the race but I did not come last. As I ran toward the finish line on the last day of the race, filthy, exhausted and elated, I was repeating the Serenity Prayer over and over in my head. For those unfamiliar with the Serenity Prayer it is the prayer used by members of Alcoholics Anonymous to underpin their twelve-step programme. As it happens I am not an advocate of the twelve-step programme but I do use the prayer and even have it tattooed on my back. It was also the prayer put on my father's mass card after he died in 1988. The prayer is a simple one.

God, grant me the serenity to accept the things I cannot change, courage to change the things I can and the wisdom to know the difference, Amen.

Running toward the finish line I got stuck on the line "courage to change the things I can" – this crazy race, this momentous effort, for me, was the moment I fully understood that I could change, not only my own life but also others'. I had the courage, now it was time for the change.

Roll on a couple of years and, sadly, like most momentous moments, my experience in the sand had become a distant memory. I only ever talked of my achievement during my work as a school speaker. All ambition of world domination had gone. Somewhere during that time I had lost ground and was falling into old habits of low self-esteem – thinking that I was not worth believing. I was stuck listening to the first part of the prayer, instead of my previously favourite second part. I was accepting the things I could not change, which, of course, was leading me to more negative thoughts, so really the whole prayer is kind of flawed.

As I stood in front of yet another group of students telling them what I'd achieved in 2010, I realised I was in danger of becoming a one hit wonder. I could see myself becoming a vaguely interesting old sort, telling the same "When I were a lad..." stories over and over again; living off one great moment – basking in my past glory while other great opportunities passed me by. I finally realised that my Sahara experience was just a small achievement and only a fraction of my capabilities, and when I use the words '*my capabilities*,' I mean those of an addict. I want my life to reflect those of addicts across the world. So, when I say completing the Marathon des Sables was only a fraction of '*my capabilities*,' I mean it is only a fraction of what we, recovering addicts, can all achieve. I believe that '*our capabilities*' have been held back for so long that my need to run across America was born out of a frustration that *we* never get told or shown what we are truly capable of. *We* are constrained by the rules of the recovery programmes we follow, or the small-minded beliefs of those who tell us we should be thankful just to be alive.

Fuck that!

I want *us* to be more and do more in the world. I want the recovering addict to be accepted, even revered as a symbol of hope and determination. To set the bar high in the lives we lead and the stories we tell, so that people without addiction will look at their own lives and realise how little they are achieving with so much. Running across the United States is me setting the standard we should all expect from ourselves, the standard which my children can aim for and, inevitably, go higher.

My run would also symbolise the daily struggle with addiction. I pictured my past addiction, as it seemed to me for so many years, as the inviting and vast crystal blue waters of the Pacific Ocean. Leaving something like that behind is difficult and even traumatic. Heading off into the mountains, like entering sobriety, leaves you feeling good, even happy, but quickly you realise that you are on your own with little or no support. You have two choices. Return to the shimmering waters of the Pacific or keep heading east towards uncertainty and the searing desert heat of Nevada. Either choice would mean hardship; one for a lifetime but the other would lead me to a new world.

CHAPTER 6
The Promise

The first day of the run was a little surreal. I woke early and felt as though I was having an out-of-body experience. Was I really about to run across America? How the hell had I got myself into this situation? A little bit of panic set in.

Over the previous few days my trust in Sean's ability had somewhat diminished after several heated arguments over his attitude to the project. Mind you, I was not taking into account the pressure he was under. He was apart from his son Jude and had travelled overseas for the first time ever (Amsterdam does not count as overseas, Sean). He was totally out of his comfort zone and being asked to live up to my high expectations. The pressure was making our violent tempers boil. I had also discovered that Sean had started smoking again.

The agreement before we left the UK was that there would be no smoking on the trip. I felt smoking gave an unhealthy image of our team. Although it was Run4Sobriety, I didn't want people thinking I was ignoring other addictions. I also detest smoking. The last thing I want to see or smell after a day of running was cigarette smoke.

A few days earlier, coming out of a phone shop having just sorted the communications for both of us, I caught Sean, like a naughty schoolboy, smoking outside the shop. Rather than try to hide it he decided to be a little bit cocky. "Put the cigarette out Sean," were my only words to him. I was expecting a confrontation but instead he sulked... Without a word he stormed off and headed for the hotel. Anyone who knows me will tell you that I don't tolerate sulking. I'm more of a scream at each other until it's resolved and then forget about it type of person. People who sulk really fall way down in my estimation. Especially grown men! After about 30 minutes of getting more annoyed I became angry. How could he do this to me? How could he put me under this amount of stress only two days before I started the biggest challenge of my life? How could he not see that the whole point of the trip was to show people how to deal with their addictions? How could he be so weak? Back at the hotel room I exploded with rage. Screaming at him to explain himself. He just looked at me weakly and made some half-arsed excuse that it was his choice. I lost it...

"You don't get this do you Sean? It's not your choice, you are only here because of Run4Sobriety, this is not a fucking holiday. This is not some lads' trip where we can just fuck off for the day and ignore the rules. This is serious stuff. I have a lot of time, my money and sponsors' money invested in this and you want to risk it all for a cigarette? What a fucking wanker you are! Why don't you just fuck off home? I'd rather do this on my own than be anywhere near you!"

With that Sean left the room and I began to think of ways to get across America without a driver.

After another half an hour I rang Zoë. I didn't know it yet but Zoë was going to be the voice of reason over the next few months. She would be the one who would give an objective opinion, usually based on fact, not my frustration. This would prove vital in the overall success of the trip. She told me to back off and to cut Sean a bit of slack. It is not in my nature to do that but I trusted Zoë's opinion and did what she told me.

We never really spoke properly about what happened that day but in the evening Sean and I agreed to make some adjustments and we would see what happened over the coming weeks. I did make it clear to him, however, that this trip and his role was about getting me across the States. There was no hidden agenda or ulterior motive. Just get me safely to New York.

I did not sleep much that night. I went over all sorts of scenarios. I couldn't let Sean know that I was dependent on him for the success of the trip, as I was worried he would use that against me when I might be physically at breaking point. I had to put on a front. I had make it seem like I would make it across with or without him. The truth was, of course, I couldn't do it without him. Had I made the wrong choice in asking him to be my support driver? Only time would tell.

Apart from the worry about Sean's abilities, I had other concerns. The pain in my knee was beginning to get to the stage of, "holy shit that hurts".

The day before the start of Run4Sobriety I decided to run in the 'Bay to Breakers'. First run in 1912, when I heard this historic seven-mile race was being held the day before my start date I knew I had to enter. How could I be in San Francisco and not take part?

I needed to go to the race expo in order to collect my number a couple of days before the race. This is always a bit of a ball ache but in races of this size I understand why they do it. To send out thirty thousand race numbers by post including the overseas runners would be a logistical nightmare as well as very costly. It's also a great opportunity for the race sponsors to get value for their investment; manning stalls, talking and selling direct to the runners is an invaluable marketing opportunity. Sean and I headed leisurely across the city, taking in the sights and sounds. There was no rush and San Francisco is a pretty amazing place – full of noise and bustle like every major city but without the rough edge of New York City or the grime of London. The 'Surfer Dude' of cities, mellow and smiling, San Francisco certainly has its own style. It felt soothing, no one seemed to be in a rush to get anywhere and it made me feel very calm. My relaxed state was short lived.

After a two-hour saunter we arrived at the expo centre to join a very, very long queue. And I thought that queuing was something only the British did! There must have been 2,000 runners waiting for the expo to open its doors. This was the last thing I needed. I was already struggling with the heat and I was worried about getting sunburn if I had to stand out for too much longer. There was nothing we could do but join the line of people. The thought of standing in line for a long period without coffee (I love coffee) was too much for Sean and I, so I dispatched him and Connor on a mission to Starbucks to get some well-earned caffeine, something that would become Sean's main job for the next 100 days. I stood in line slowly making my way forwards, desperate in my attempts to avoid conversations or eye contact.

Despite my outward confidence I can become very shy and completely hopeless in certain situations. I really have to work hard to lower my barriers and I am not good at initiating conversations with strangers – at least not when I am sober and I often used my shyness as an excuse to drink more. Meanwhile, back in the sun-baked queue I tried to act 'normally' in my uncomfortable way, but eventually my worst fears were realised when someone spoke to me. OK, so it was not that bad but it did make me feel a little queasy inside. This older gentleman asked me how far I had travelled to do the Bay to Breakers. He was a little stunned when I told him I had travelled from the UK. "Man that's a long way to travel for a seven-mile race," I smiled and then told him the full story of what I was about to do, "You are going to run from San Francisco to where? New York City!" he was stunned for the second time. After a short silence he asked what everyone does, "Why?" I explained about my battle with alcohol and my aim to raise more awareness of recovery from addiction. There was a third stunned silence. At this point I thought, here we go another judgemental idiot who hasn't a clue what I'm talking about when I heard the jingle jangle of coins. Out of his pocket the man produced several coins, they were in fact sobriety chips. These chips or coins are usually given to Alcoholics Anonymous members and represent the length of time that person has stayed sober. "My name is Jan and I am nineteen years sober, I always carry these chips to remind myself of my struggle." A fourth silence but this time I was the stunned one. Of all the people in the line I could have been next to, I was next to a fellow, recovering addict.

Wow, the conversation began to flow and we shared our joint love of all things running and recovery. When Sean and Connor returned there was a little disbelief before they too joined into this wonderful moment. As the doors opened the queue began to shorten and I actually wanted it to slow down, so I could savour time with Jan. Finally, we reached the entrance, we shook hands and said our goodbyes.

What a moment. As I picked up my number my mind was going over what had happened in the line. How? Why? I was in a bit of a fluster when Jan returned and asked if he could have a photograph with us. I was more than happy to oblige. As we had our picture taken he pulled one of his sobriety chips. "Would you take this chip with you Tom and promise me to throw it in the Atlantic when you get there?" I was totally blown away by Jan's faith in me. He had no doubts about my ability to complete the trip. He had entrusted me with his hard-earned sobriety coin and his faith. It was a huge honour for me to do this for him, for this complete stranger, for my sobriety brother.

The race itself was a real eye-opener. I had managed to get to the start line with very little hassle, just three miles from my hotel. It was also an early start so I left Sean and Connor to sleep. On arriving I was greeted by a naked runner with only a Barack Obama mask on, carrying an American flag. A little much for seven a.m. in the morning. The atmosphere was building as the crowd got bigger and bigger. I hoped I would bump into Jan but quickly realised that the likelihood of that happening was very remote. As start time approached, for some unknown reason people, started throwing fajita wraps. This looked pretty funny but not something I would be participating in. Even when one landed on my shoulder and a fellow runner asked, "Hey man, are you going to throw it?"

I smiled politely, as I took it off my shoulder and threw it to the floor. "Where I come from we don't do that sort of shit." I was pleased that my miserable mindset had not yet been punctured by that indomitable Californian happiness... well, at least not yet.

The race was like any other although a little tougher than I would have liked the day before a run across a continent (think San Francisco, think hills...). But it had great atmosphere and an even better finish, right beside that blue and shiny Pacific Ocean. I was pleased I ran the Bay to Breakers and, if you get the chance, I would heartily recommend it.

The only issue I had that day was the return from the finish line. Instead of being sensible and catching a bus back into San Francisco I decided to walk. I didn't realise that this was going to be an additional 10 miles, taking my mileage total for the day to 20. But, it did mean that I met Laura Ku, who was very helpful with directions from the finish line and great company as we walked back towards the city. Laura was also to meet me at the finish line in New York City 100 days later, which was so totally cool. I am very thankful for her friendship. I arrived back at the hotel sometime after lunch, totally shattered. Not my smartest planning but hey, it wasn't going to be the last day I would suffer!

Boy did I pay for that day. Having an injury was never going to stop me from starting this challenge. The fear was would the injury stop me from *finishing* the challenge? You can be bullish to your friends and family about your own ability but deep down you know your own body. I was in a lot of pain and I honestly did not think my knee was going to last the first week let alone 100 days. I tried to push the pain to the back of my mind.

Heading down for breakfast I felt sick. I always suffer from pre-race nerves but this was different; this was not a race. I was about to start a new way of life. I was about to face the hardest challenge of my life. How the heck was I going to eat anything? Thankfully, this is America and the breakfast buffet was full of pastries and pancakes – I always manage to eat sweet stuff even when I'm feeling sick. Knowing that I would burn approximately 3,500 calories per day meant that I didn't feel so bad about stuffing my face with as many pastries as I could, followed by pancakes covered in maple syrup. About 5,000 calories later and a gallon of coffee (have I mentioned that I love coffee?) I was ready to get my stuff and head to the iconic Golden Gate Bridge and my personal start line.

This was my first chance to see Sean's driving in action. Surprisingly it was pretty smooth and we navigated our way from Fisherman's Wharf to the car park of the Golden Gate Bridge in less than 20 minutes. My plan was to start at nine a.m. I had somehow convinced myself that someone might turn up to wish me well. I waited until the last moment. No one did. We took photographs and had a group prayer. I checked my phone, which was to be my constant companion and Jan's sobriety chip, safe, deep in my pocket.

I remember thinking "life is never going to be the same again." Was that a bad thing? No, was it fuck a bad thing, it was a bloody fantastic thing! I wanted my life to change, I wanted every bit of who I was to change. I was going to embrace every difficult moment.

With no ceremony, without looking back, I began to run.

Leaving the Golden Gate Bridge, I made my way down onto the water front and followed the water's edge for about four miles. It was a fantastic feeling running alongside the San Francisco Bay with the big bridge behind me and a view of Alcatraz in front, it was one of those once in a lifetime moments that you dream of. Every now and again I would remind myself that I was running across the whole of America and this sobering thought instantly brought me back to the job at hand, which was to finish each day strong enough to run again the next.

My first checkpoint was below the Bay Bridge. The Bay Bridge is a fantastic structure with a double motorway carrying 260,000 vehicles per day. Sadly, it doesn't allow pedestrians, so we made this my first stop, I refilled with water and we drove over the bridge, so that I could find a safe place to resume my run. Now, before anyone says, "You didn't run all of the USA!" yes I did, I just didn't run over all the bridges that cross water. That's just part of the deal and if anyone has a problem with that, tough!

Having crossed the Bay Bridge we pulled into a petrol station (in the States they are gas stations and pavements are sidewalks – seems only right to call them that from now on) to establish a route. Most people who decide to run across America would have been studying maps for weeks and months to ensure they had a firm grasp of the direction they were heading. Not me. I had left Zoë to do the maps and thought it would be easy to log on to the website and follow the route she had planned out. In principle that was a great idea. In reality it was probably the dumbest idea I had ever had. If you are ever going to do this type of thing please heed this warning. **KNOW YOUR ROUTE** and **DON'T RELY ON WI-FI** (was that in a loud enough font?)

We had no internet connection, therefore we could not access the route, therefore we didn't have a clue which road we should be on. I'd only run seven miles and we were lost. What a dickhead! How embarrassing, I was a team leader and I didn't know which direction I was going. Thankfully, I am quite decisive and quickly found a road that would keep us in the right direction for the rest of the day. San Pablo Avenue took us from the outskirts of Oakland through Berkeley and up into Richmond. It also took us through some tough neighbourhoods. This was giving me a taste of what was in store for the rest of the run. I was not going to be running continually through the tourist, picture postcard parts of America, I would often be running through the reality of a country struggling with poverty, addiction and dispossession – just like so many others around the world.

As the heat of the day rose to a nice 27 degrees I remembered how much I hate heat. I live in Yorkshire in the North of England, so heat is not something I encounter that often. Even when the sun does come out I will sit and wait for dusk before going out on my daily runs. I don't perform well in sunshine – a friend once described the sun as

'Irish Kryptonite'. I would definitely agree with this. I felt myself getting weaker and weaker. My hat was on along with a bandana and sunblock on my skin but I seriously felt like I was burning up. Sean, Connor and I had agreed to meet up in a shopping plaza car park where I was to get a taste of the food that lay ahead. A big cheese and ham sandwich with a bag of crisps – it was like being back at school. I tried to get into some shade but it was impossible to cool down. It was time to suck it up and enjoy the ride. Enduring temperatures like this is impossible to allow for when you live in the UK. I had to acclimatise as quickly as possible and ensure I kept on top of my hydration. Thankfully, I decided to use a hydration pack, which turned out to be my most essential piece of kit. Being able to carry two litres of fluid in these temperatures and higher was vital to my ability to finish each day.

After a 30-minute break I got back on the road. I had already started to stiffen up even though I had only stopped for a short period. My pace had slowed dramatically and all sorts of doubts entered my head. I wasn't fit enough for this. I was not prepared physically or mentally. My team were not strong enough. We may as well go home. All negative feelings that, if you allow them, will eventually destroy you. They had to be put to one side.

As I ran I remembered an email I received from Gerry Duffy. Gerry is an awesome endurance athlete from Ireland. He wrote:

"Perhaps though I might send my most empowering learning: gratitude. If I ever doubt myself or have a hard mental moment or two, I go there. I remind myself how lucky I am to have the health that I do and that I do these events by ambition. I don't have to do them, I get to. It always works."

These words were so true. I had chosen to be in this situation. I was lucky to be in this situation. I was happy to have the ambition to succeed; all I needed now was a pair of balls! Once my head was sorted the rest of the day went off pretty smoothly. At 28 miles I reached yet another bridge where Sean and Connor were waiting. It was a big relief to finish

CHAPTER 7

California

 FB post 20 May 2013 Laura Ku
Good Luck! It was great to meet you after Bay2Breakers.

that first day and head for our first taste of motel life.

Like most things in life getting started is always the most difficult part of any task and finishing that first day was a big relief. Take this book – it took me over a month just to write the first page. Gradually, it became easier and, like most challenges, at the end of my first day I sincerely hoped that's how the run would go.

Making our way out of Valejo we headed east on Highway 29 towards the Napa Valley. Ironic that Run4Sobriety would be winding its way through one of the biggest wine regions in America, interestingly though, even during my heaviest drinking days I disliked wine, but what a beautiful place to run though.

With the urban sprawl of San Francisco, Oakland and Valejo behind us the most wonderful rolling hills and countryside opened out. The downside to this was we lost all sidewalks. Sidewalks in the States are a nightmare. In the cities there are plenty but once you hit a town they are sporadic. They will run for 500 metres and then just stop. It's as though no one walks in America. That surely cannot be true… can it?

In the countryside you can forget about sidewalks altogether – you are on your own. All I had for company was a white line and a hard shoulder about a half metre wide between me and the traffic, including big trucks doing 60 miles per hour.

Sean and Connor had found a place to park up just before lunch. As they waited for me to arrive they drew the attention of a highway patrol police officer. Yes guys a proper 'CHiPS' moment (who is old enough to remember the 70s NBC show?). Officer Warrington pulled up on the biggest kick ass Harley Davidson any of us had ever seen. He approached Sean to ask him if there was a problem with his car and by Officer Warrington's reaction, it was possibly the first time Sean was able to grasp the scale of what we were trying to achieve. "What? Your brother is running across the United States? Is he crazy?"

Thankfully, to back up the story I arrived at the checkpoint. It was great to see that this police officer, who had probably seen it all, was so enthusiastic about our journey. He talked to me about the route and also the importance of getting the message of sobriety out there; he knew the scale of alcoholism in the States was at epidemic proportions. I could hear in his voice a genuine desire for us to succeed. This spurred me on. I had been quite down after the struggles of the first day, so, starting to get our message out was a big confidence boost. After having some photos taken and a last discussion about our route, he took off. What a cool guy.

My route led me onto Highway 12 and my first dice with American road works. I have worked in the UK road works industry for over 20 years and pedestrian safety is one of the highest priorities. We ensure that if a pedestrian enters our works they can safely find a route around or through. In the US it is a completely different attitude. As there are no pedestrians, and I truly mean that, outside the city NO ONE walks anywhere, the need for pedestrian safety is non-existent.

As I approached I was already getting strange looks from the road workers. They were probably thinking who is this nut job walking along the highway? I asked if I could walk through the site and was told, no, it was too dangerous, but frankly, it wasn't half as dangerous as running on the highway with no hard shoulder! I may as well have been speaking

Dutch as one workman just shrugged his shoulders and continued what he was doing. I decided to carry on. The road works went on for about six miles and it was my first taste of abuse from the drivers of America. "Feck you!" I thought, I'm allowed on the highway too, so I'm going to hold my ground. That attitude, however, does not work for trucks. They do not give a damn about your rights and I had to swallow my pride a few times as I leapt into the ditch for safety. I knew that I had to toughen up to the challenges ahead. The roads would become busier, although I was not expecting what happened next.

At the end of Highway 12, instead of an intersection, the highway simply merged with the mighty I-80 (the transcontinental highway that runs from San Francisco across to Teaneck, New Jersey) I was effectively running on the US equivalent of the M1! I don't think I have ever run that fast. For about half a mile I had trucks and cars blasting their horns for me to get off the interstate. It was pretty scary stuff. I eventually got to the next exit and safety. Running on the I-80 was not in the script.

The plan for the journey was to only think about one state at a time. I figured that we could just about manage to think about the journey in bite-size chunks and we had a firm rule: no one talks about New York. The words New York became like Voldemort from the Harry Potter movies – strictly forbidden. If you mention it bad things will happen. I was pretty happy with this in the early stages. Being able to focus on South Lake Tahoe, which was the last town in California, gave me something to aim for. It was manageable.

As I made my way toward South Lake I went through various towns including Fairfield and Davis. Pretty, standard towns, nothing spectacular – a big main street with a large government building taking centre stage. Like a more modern version of the western towns seen in the movies. I imagine many of these towns haven't changed much since then! Having been spoilt in San Francisco with so many iconic landmarks it was nice to see 'normal'. Davis was a little bit quirky, as they have their own cycle network, complete with dedicated roundabouts for the cycling rush hour. The landscape, by this stage, was now flat and rural – nothing much going on apart from a few truck whizzing past my head.

As I left Davis I could see the skyline of Sacramento, the first big city since San Francisco. I love seeing the skyline of a big city for the first time. It fills me with excitement. What is it going to be like, am I going to be blown away by its size, is it going to be tough or cosmopolitan? Are the buildings going to be old or new? Is there going to be a mixture of both? Are the people going to be friendly or rude?

The first time I got excited about a skyline like this was in 1995 when I arrived in Sydney, Australia, for the first time. I had managed to get work digging trenches for fibre optic cables in downtown Sydney. It was an early start of 5 a.m. so it was still dark when I was picked up. As we drove the freeway into the city the sun was just coming up. I caught my first glimpse of Sydney. Wow! Had I not been in a van with a rough-arsed Paddy I think I would have burst into tears. It was such a beautiful sight and a memory that has stayed with me all these years.

I got the same tingle down my spine as Sacramento's spectacular outline rose up, sitting proudly in the distance with nothing surrounding it. I couldn't wait to see what it had in store for me.

On the map there was no road between Davis and Sacramento apart from the I-80. I had been stressing about this for a few days. "How the hell can there be no other roads into the city. Surely people must ride their bikes into work?" I took a gamble and headed back toward the dreaded interstate. I was in luck. Rather than build a road for a few cyclists the authorities decided it would be easier to use the hard shoulder as the cycle/run lane and had installed large concrete blocks and fencing to partition the pedestrians and the interstate traffic; however, I am not sure that really is protection for anyone if a truck or car slammed into you. What felt like another headlong dash by the massive four-lane interstate was quite an experience and I was pretty glad to reach the suburbs of Sacramento.

The vast city did not disappoint. I met the scruffy, poverty stricken suburbs on the west of town. This was something I needed to get to grips with, the dispossessed, the sour reflection of the American dream that I saw first hand over the following three months did and still does, make me angry. Drawn further into the city and things started to change. Clean sidewalks, gleaming office blocks, the whole place felt brand new. I saw my first ball park and state Capitol building. All very American – it changed my mood and made me feel great. The energy was fantastic. I made it to the checkpoint to find Sean and Connor relaxing under a tree. The looked happy. I'd struggled all day, the heat had been ridiculous and seeing my crew laughing and joking lifted my mood a little.

I think at this point I need to make one thing clear about heat; I hate it! I had been spoilt with the cooling Pacific breeze in San Francisco, now the further away from the coast we went the more intense the heat would get. I was a long way off the heat of Nevada and Kansas, which is brutal, but I was still struggling. The hottest day had been 27 degrees, a pleasant summer's afternoon for some, in fact I saw many Californians wearing jumpers. All I had on was a t-shirt and shorts and if I thought I could have got away with running naked I think I would have seriously considered it. Ever since my early days as a child in Ireland I have feared the sun. Having been badly sunburnt several times the sun was like the devil to me. As soon as it appeared I went inside. Even whilst working in Australia in the 1990s I hated every minute of having the sun beating down on me. This would prove a real difficulty. I was not someone who ran well in the sun and therefore it was yet another obstacle to get over. As the mercury soared that day coming into Sacramento I can assure you I was already feeling beaten.

Connor joined me for the last four miles of the day. We chatted about all sort of things. I enjoyed his company; it had been a lonely first 48 hours.

My first taste of old school America was Placerville with its nickname "Old Hangtown"!

"Why do they call it Old Hangtown?" "Because we used to hang people and lots of 'em."

Placerville was a one street town. All original looking buildings from around 1870, it had a real classic feel to it and was the first sign of the famous Pony Express. When we planned the trip I was fascinated by the Pony Express.

"The Pony Express was a mail service delivering messages, newspapers, mail, even small packages from St. Joseph, Missouri across the Great Plains, over the Rocky Mountains and the Sierra Nevada to Sacramento, California by horseback, using a series of relay stations. During its 18 months of operation, it reduced the time for messages to travel between the Atlantic and Pacific coasts to about ten days. From April 3, 1860 to October 1861, it became the West's most direct means of east–west communication before the telegraph was established and was vital for tying the new state of California with the rest of the country." Wikipedia.

The skill and bravery of the riders and horses, the solitude and hardships they endured give Pony Express a romantic feel. In reality I am sure it was a tough job. I was to find out how tough the terrain was over the next month. To be able to follow in the footsteps of these pioneers was a tremendous honour for me. Although my route would be on paved roads and I would have the luxury of a support vehicle I would still get a taste of the physical hardship facing those men. I would be able to understand the temperatures and the terrain. I would see the wildlife and the unchanged scenery. Not so much my 'moon landing' as my 'back to the future' moment!

Back in Placerville, Sean and Connor decided to go shopping and came back with a bewildering array of tourist tat. It turns out Sean can be made to buy anything with a little pressure from a woman in a cowboy hat. Thankfully Connor saw sense and took some of the shit back for a refund.

As the temperature started to rise towards the 30-degree mark we took our first split day. This involved taking time off during the afternoon and going out to finish the day's mileage later in the cooler evening. The hottest time seemed to be between 2 p.m. and 6 p.m. so we decided to finish at 3 p.m. and go back out at 6.30 p.m. This was not going to be possible every day due to hotel locations, but where we could, we adopted this system. Even for Sean and Connor, forced to sit waiting for me at checkpoints inside the car during those peak temperatures was beyond ridiculous.

Sitting in a motel room during the afternoon felt a little bit strange at first – like I was cheating. I knew, however, if I was to succeed I needed to be super smart at protecting my body. Rest, food and the right amount of fluid was vital. During these afternoon breaks I would try not to sleep but would just relax and eat. Anyone walking into my motel room would have thought, "Jeez, he doesn't look like an athlete!" as I sprawled across a bed strewn with McDonald's wrappers, a can of a Dr Pepper and maybe some spilt M&Ms – I probably looked more like some unemployed drop-out.

In the evening Connor again agreed to join me for the last six or seven miles of the day. I really did enjoy my time with Connor. Even though he would hate to hear it there are real similarities between him and me when I was 18. Thankfully, he doesn't have the unbridled rage I struggled with at his age. What he does have is a belief that he is going to succeed. I often thought that I wouldn't make the mistakes my role models made. But, I did! I made all the same mistakes. I know that Connor will make mistakes too and it frustrates me that he can't see what's in front of him, but putting an old head on young shoulders is impossible and it's what makes him who he is.

We made our way from the motel up towards Camino climbing into the El Dorado hills. It was a beautiful evening. I remember stopping Connor and encouraging him to really take in the landscape. The El Dorado hills were not the biggest I had ever seen but there was something special about them. There was a rolling beauty with crystal blue skies as a backdrop – the deep orange glow of the setting sun was casting long shadows over the peaks like a blanket being pulled up for the night. It was a memorable sunset that evening and, as we approached the top of a hill we came across a church.

Most of the churches in America have boards outside with scripture written on them and I found them very uplifting throughout my journey. This particular church board proclaimed:

"Awake you who sleep and Christ will give you light." Eph5:14

I loved this, as all evening I had been talking to Connor about my journey of faith. He seemed sceptical. Reading these words almost spoke to him, although he won't admit it. I hope one day he will awake and realise that Christ is with him. Sorry, I will try to limit the church and faith references... no, I won't really.

The end of the evening's run finished outside a general store in Camino. Connor and I were both shattered after a long, hot day on the road and as we sat and waited for Sean to collect us, both enjoying a can of ice-cold coke, some locals approached and asked what we had been doing. When I explained I was running for awareness of addiction they smiled and sat down to tell us their story, one, which sadly, I was to hear again and again... A continuous battle between alcohol and crystal meth, several rehab attempts only to find themselves battling again in their neighbourhoods to find a way out of the despair of poverty and isolation. Almost a sense of it's a shit world made a little better through drugs and alcohol. I was happy to hear one of the women say that she had stayed sober for over a year despite her partner's continued struggle. Her partner was trying and I respected him for that. He just didn't have the strength for the final push and I still pray that he finds it. Sean arrived and joined the conversation. It was important that we had conversations like this, as it reinforced what we were doing and why. Slowly we were becoming a solid unit with a determination to spread the message of sobriety and recovery.

Camino was kind to us. I felt a real connection with the people we met that night. It would continue the next day too. I began as usual – a nice steady four miles before I had my first stop. Connor had decided to join me for the first stint of the day. Sean had driven up the road to find a good place for breakfast.

After pulling into the car park of a large diner Sean got chatting to one of the owners and, of course, they got talking about the run. The man told Sean that there was to be a meeting of Narcotics Anonymous at 11 a.m. on the patio of the diner. Sean couldn't believe it. Of all the places to stop he had managed to find a place where our journey would really be appreciated.

When we met at the next checkpoint I was shocked and delighted by the coincidence too but, it was only 9.30 a.m., staying on would seriously impact on the day. It would put me behind on my mileage. Frustratingly, I was already missing my daily target of 33 miles. Rather than my usual quick reactionary decision-making, I chose to take some time to think. It suddenly occurred to me that I was being a complete idiot, already blinded by my own needs instead of thinking of of others. *So what* I would be behind on my mileage, *so what* if we had to run later into the night. This was a gift. It was an opportunity to be with my people, to listen and to share our journeys. We stayed for the meeting. Sean, Connor and I were deeply moved by the stories we heard and by the people we met. During that morning, after hearing about my meeting with Jan, a man called Carey put his sobriety chip into my hand. He too showed more faith in me than I had in myself – a truly humbling thing for me to experience. It would be an honour to carry his chip alongside Jan's to the Atlantic. The support the group showed us that day and over the next three months was phenomenal! I want to thank them all and hope that one day I will be back with them.

Keep the faith guys.

The mileage that day was tough but made so much easier with the group's support. I was now running over the iconic Sierra Nevada Mountains. These mountains were the last barrier for the pioneers from the east during the Gold Rush of 1849. Many people perished making their way across them in harsh winter conditions. Thankfully, I was making the journey in better weather with a lot less risk. It was still going to my toughest test to date and my first real taste of steep climbs. Surrounded by the towering pine forest of the Yosemite National Park, the scenery was spectacular. So much so, that I managed to fall flat on my face at the side of the highway. It's always embarrassing falling over. It bloody hurt as well. Luckily there was no real harm done apart from a bit of a graze on my knee.

One day's run from reaching South Lake Tahoe and my feet were really taking a pounding. The blisters I had expected but the swelling I had not. You always know that your feet will suffer and swell a little – maybe half a size. My feet had already grown one size bigger and I could no longer get my feet into my new trainers. Due to a lack of funds I only had two new pairs of trainers and my old pair of Asics. Luckily, I had bought a cheap pair of New Balance in San Francisco that were a size bigger than I needed. Boy, was I glad I did. The blisters I had developed had become so painful I was now struggling to go much faster than a walk. At one stage I had a blister under a blister. It was beyond anything I'd ever experienced before – I have had blisters, but not to this extent. Even when I ran the Marathon des Sables my feet were sore but not so bad I couldn't run. My New Balance trainers took a real pounding and were really not up to what I needed. The lack of cushioning at the back of the shoe was causing more swelling on my heel and that was leading to yet more blisters. I just needed to make it to Lake Tahoe and I'm sure I would find a sports store that could sort me out (or so I thought). Before I could get to South Lake Tahoe there was a small matter of Echo Summit – my first big mountain climb.

Now, Ben Nevis, the tallest mountain in Great Britain, rises to 4,409ft above sea level. Echo Summit is a climb to 7,382ft – this will also give you some idea of the scale of the Sierra Nevada. This is not to say that climbing Ben Nevis is easy, it's not. Echo Summit is just a damn site taller.

At the bottom of the climb it was bright sunshine and warm; however, it changed very quickly and within about an hour I was faced with a very fine mist turning to rain. It was bloody awful. The rain wasn't torrential but it was the sort that gets you wet – the stuff your mother would warn you about.

For the first hour I will be honest I loved it. I'm Irish, I love rain (it's not called the Emerald Isle for nothing). After the previous two weeks of baking sunshine I was glad of the cooler conditions. I was pleased my pasty white Irish skin wasn't being scorched yet again. But, after three hours of climbing the mountain, being soaked by speeding cars and trucks, I had had enough. The wet weather was playing havoc with my blisters and I was getting cold. True tests are something that I think we all shy away from. Too often when faced with adversity we turn away. I had nowhere to turn. I had to get to the top.

Getting angry is something that has often got me into trouble in the past. I have a bad temper. It is under control but every now and again I need to call on that anger to get me through certain situations. This was one of those situations. As I climbed closer to the top, soaked to the skin, skinless raw feet, getting colder and colder, I began to ask why did I have to do this? *Why* were alcoholics and drug addicts being treated so badly? *Why* wasn't there a national day of sobriety? *Why* do people think it's still OK to judge an addict just because they think they are better than them? No one is better than me! I truly mean that! Not in an egotistical way but as a human being, I believe that no one is better than me. In the same way that I am not better than anyone else. We are all children of God. Do not fucking judge me unless you are ready for a fight.

I had got myself into a real emotional frenzy. I powered up the last few miles of the mountain fuelled by anger and determination. Seeing the sign at the summit was a great feeling. There to greet me, Sean and Connor both smiled as I took the photo at the top. I had done it. I had shown all the doubters that I would never give up. I had shown everyone that recovering addicts can do fantastic things! After about ten minutes I came back down to earth, as I remembered that I still had another 10 miles to run that day. With little energy left and all my adrenaline used up on the climb the pain kicked in.

The wet conditions had torn my feet to bits. The searing pain had become almost unbearable. I had been looking forward to the downhill section into Tahoe. I was hoping to make up some time by running the final 10 miles but I hardly managed a walk. At one stage I contemplated taking my shoes off all together to allow my feet some respite but feared not being able to get them back on again. Those last 10 miles took me another four hours. I felt like a broken man but I had reached the last town before the state line. One down, 13 to go ...

CHAPTER 8
Nevada

2,809.29 miles to go
Battle born

South Lake Tahoe, not the nicest of places, looked a little like I felt, tired. The Lake however was spectacular. Back home, I'm lucky to live in the beautiful county of Yorkshire in England. Often referred to as 'God's Own County', the scenery around us is something to behold and I am very proud that I live in such a stunning place. Even with home on my mind, arriving on the edge of Lake Tahoe I was completely blown away by its sheer size and beauty. Yorkshire can't touch this! I rang Sean and Connor to meet me so that we could share the experience together. None of us had seen anything like it. It was almost mystical and a hard spot to leave. Often on the trip I would have to remind myself that I was not a tourist. I wasn't able to spend time taking pictures or marvelling at the beauty of the surroundings. I had to keep moving. Leaving the lake was made even tougher by the knowledge that I was heading into the most inhospitable land imaginable. I was crossing the state line into Nevada.

During all the planning for the trip most of my focus was on Nevada. I almost became obsessed by it. I spent hours and hours just looking at pictures of long, deserted, heat-baked roads and I was about to see it, to feel it for the first time. Nevada's nickname is the Battle Born State because it joined the union during the Civil War and I knew I certainly had a battle ahead.

Crossing over my first state line was a bit of an anti-climax. There was only a tiny little sign saying 'Nevada State Line'. It meant so much to me yet drivers and pedestrians were paying it no attention. I ran along the lake edge, which was surrounded by the most beautiful big houses built into the mountainside with fantastic balcony views of Lake Tahoe, and began to climb up into the hills and over Spooner Summit rising up at 7,146ft.

Despite a new pair of trainers from a sports store in South Lake my feet were still in pretty bad shape. The heat of the day caused swelling and, even though my new shoes were size 11.5 (one and half sizes bigger than normal), I was still struggling. Made worse by the previous day's rain-soaked miles, the blisters on my feet were very sore. My ankles too were just one big blister and I now had a blister under another blister between my toes, caused by my usually faithful toe socks. I had worn this particular brand of sock, Injiji, in many UK races, but my swollen feet had caused them to rub. I was fast discovering that what kit worked in the UK may not stand the test in the US. My method of dealing with blisters was to take a big slice of 'man up' pie and burst them with my trusty pin, covered them in antiseptic cream and hope for the best. They would toughen up eventually... I hoped. Thankfully, the beauty of the summit and subsequent run down towards Carson City took away some of the pain. I could literally see mountain ranges for hundreds of miles. It was breath-taking. Suddenly, it occurred to me, "Holy shit I have to run over those mountains!" It was going to be a love/hate relationship.

In order to prepare for what was ahead I made the decision to take a day off in Carson City. My feet were trashed and Sean and Connor looked as though they needed some R&R. So I bedded down in a Motel 6 room for the day whilst Sean and Connor went off to see the sights. I enjoyed the peace and quiet after the constant anxiety of traffic hurtling past my head for the previous ten days. I just lay in bed thinking of the journey ahead, whilst eating M&Ms and drinking Gatorade. It was a strange combination but it made me feel better. I will probably never again visit Carson City but I could not waste energy sightseeing. Rest days had to be exactly that.

I had decided a long time ago that my route would include Highway 50. Infamous for a variety of reasons, the Highway follows the route of the old Pony Express and the Lincoln Highway, named after, arguably, America's most popular president Abraham Lincoln. But the reason I chose to run Highway 50 was because of an article in *Life* magazine that called it the loneliest road in America. Written in July 1986, the article described the Highway, and rural Nevada, as a place devoid of civilisation. I was facing 17 mountain passes and, from the town of Fallon to Delta in Utah, there were only three small towns in a distance of just over 400 miles. To most people it would sound like hell on earth. To me it sounded like addiction; so many things between success and failure; so many reasons to say I can't do it; it was exactly the test I needed to show the tough choices an addict faces every day. Highway 50 was built for me.

Before I hit the loneliest road section I made my way from Carson City along the highway to Fallon. My first real stretch of long straight road. The temperature had been steadily rising as I made my way further east and was hitting thirty degrees on a regular basis, I loved the challenge. I had been refreshed by my day off and had even managed to speak to one of my oldest friends, Andy Turton. Andy had called me in Carson City and gave me a real morale boost. Us Yorkshire men are not known for being emotional but Andy was very clear that he was proud of me and that he knew I could do it. It meant so much to hear those words. I was 100% focused and I needed to be.

FB post 26 May 2013 Mark Brown
Tom it was sure nice meeting you today! Wishing you safe travels on your journey!

As we moved between towns, motels were becoming scarce and we had our first night of camping on a beach on the shores of a large lake. We managed to find a quiet spot away from the noise of the traffic and we had a great feed courtesy of chef Sean, despite a ferocious wind, which nearly blew our tent away. After hammering in the tent pegs we were treated to a star-gazing frenzy as the night sky got brighter and brighter with millions of sparkling stars. Without light pollution the sky at night is a magnificent sight. We spent hours talking and marvelling at the sheer scale of the universe. It got a little deep if I'm honest and I just wanted to sleep.

Leaving Fallon behind we pushed east on the loneliest road with majestic mountains ranges all around us and a wide expanse of dusty, hot parched land in front of us; we were, to be truthful, completely shitting ourselves. The road seemed to go on forever, this would surely break me – would I survive? Breaking down or running out of petrol were concerns for Sean and Connor. I was more anxious about being knocked down. We had made no emergency plans. As a matter of fact I don't even think I discussed first aid experience with either of them. It never occurred to me that something bad would happen to any of us – I'm the kind of person who is reluctant to buy travel insurance. Watching a recent programme about sportsman and adventurer James Cracknell has made me re-think future expeditions. James was hit by a truck early one morning whilst riding his bike and nearly died. It was only thanks to the driver stopping and calling the emergency services that he survived, but thanks to T-Mobile we were heading into the unknown without a mobile phone signal. Looking back it was pretty dangerous but that's how I plan things (or not) – I try to stay positive and not prepare for death.

Almost immediately I knew why it was called the loneliest road. The car count dropped almost as soon as we left Fallon. The traffic had gone and so had civilisation. There was nothing but a straight tarmac ribbon disappearing into a heat haze on the horizon.

The first section took me through Salt Well Basin, which was almost completely flat. The wide expanse of sand looked like the bottom of a prehistoric lake and boy was it hot. The afternoon temperature hit 38 °C/100°F. It felt like my feet were melting into the black, shimmering tarmac. This was not a normal heat, there was little or no breeze and when the wind did get up it was like having a hair dryer blowing in your face. My sunblock was doing a great job but essential pieces of kit were a bandana, a sun visor and my Adidas Clima-cool sun glasses. I had used these glasses in the Sahara and with the category 4 lenses they were as strong a protection as I could get for my eyes. I became a little obsessed with covering up. I had heard horror stories of people having the top of their head scorched by the sun and I didn't want this to happen to me. At every checkpoint I soaked my bandana in ice-cold water but although it was refreshing for a while it was dry within ten minutes. This was dry heat. I didn't sweat, or at least I didn't feel the sweat. As soon as I took my back pack off though you could see the salt tide mark on my t-shirt. Importantly, my hydration was spot on. This was something I had promised to get right. I was responsible for my own hydration. I had messed this up in previous races early in my running career and I had also witnessed first hand had how bad it can be.

In 2010, during the Marathon des Sables across the Sahara for a time I ran with a guy from Finland. He was a runner built like me with quite a big frame (not fat just 'big boned'). We chatted for a while and discussed our strategy for the rest of the race. He said he wanted to be the first Finnish person to complete the race. An awesome ambition I thought. I wished him well and told him to stay safe. He ran on ahead at a very fast pace. At the next checkpoint I saw him taking shelter looking exhausted. "Hey dude, it's only day one, take it easy or you won't finish at all," I said, even though I felt unqualified to give advice, I could see he was about my level of fitness and I was struggling. He didn't say a word, just charged out of the checkpoint looking like he wanted to prove a point. The next time I saw him he was surrounded by medics with a drip in his arm. He had run through two checkpoints without taking on any fluids. His race was over.

I could not afford to put myself in a similar situation and Sean was on 'pee' watch to ensure I wasn't becoming dehydrated. It is not the most glamorous job in the world watching someone else pee but it is an important one. Yellow pee with a strong smell is a warning sign of dehydration; ideally Sean wanted to see a clear stream with little smell. At every feed station I topped up my hydration pack and added electrolyte tablets, as the salt I was losing was evident on my t-shirt at the end of each day. I may not have got top marks for expedition planning but at no stage over the three months did I ever forget the importance of hydration. My pee was perfect – good enough to drink!

Our first stop was a campsite called Sand Mountain and it was exactly that, a big mountain of sand. It was like being back in the Sahara. Campsites in the US are geared up for big RVs or recreation vehicles, not real campers. Before leaving for the US I had visions in my head of soft lush grass to pitch our tent on every evening. No way! We were always on the roughest stoniest piece of shit ground they could find. Great if you were staying in a $50k dollar RV but bloody awful if you are sleeping in a small tent! The toilets too were usually fly-infested shitholes. Having worked in the construction game for over 20 years I thought I could cope with most things, but those toilets had to be seen to be believed; having a squat at the side of the road was fast becoming my preferred option.

It's all character building I would hear people say but, do you know what, I didn't want to rough it all the way across the USA, that was never the deal. The run was hard enough without having to sleep on rocks and crap outside – Bear Grylls I am not! It was, however, part of Nevada and there was no one out there to complain to.

I always struggled after a night sleeping in the tent. No shower or washing facilities of any sort left me feeling stale and grimy; not that anyone could smell me – there was no one around, yet, keeping motivated out in the middle of a desert was tough. I called upon my greatest supporter for help. I spoke to God.

My faith had grown stronger over the past 12 months but I still struggled with the 'praying out loud' part or the 'praying directly to God' carry on. I was brought up as a Catholic and the only prayers I spoke were prayers written down by others. 'Our Father', 'Hail Mary' etc. and if we wanted an intervention from God himself you had to speak to a priest who would take that job on and report back his findings. OK, so I'm being a little flippant about the Catholic Church there, but that is pretty much how it works. Having joined Life Church I discovered another way, a more direct relationship with God and it has completely changed my life and my faith.

Joining Life Church had taken a monumental shift in my thought process on Christianity. I had never talked in public about my faith, even to other parishioners at my local church. My belief system was very confused. I don't think I had ever fully understood the role of God in my dad's death and my subsequent descent into alcoholism. I think I had blamed God, as lots of people do, for all my problems.

It was only after a chance meeting with Semi Tadulala that I even knew about Life Church. He came to my house after he had read a blog I had written about my relationship with God. I think he knew I was lost and needed saving. After 45 minutes talking about everything from rugby to family, Semi asked if he could pray with me. I thought he was going to say the Lord's Prayer and begin with 'Our Father' but I was wrong. He put his hand on my shoulder and showed me the true power of prayer. As he spoke the words asking for me to be guided through my depression and addiction, I began to feel overwhelmed with emotion. I had finally found the connection with Christ I had been looking for. It was going to be good to have faith back in my life.

I was quite enjoying my morning prayer session. Being on the open road with no one for hundreds of miles meant I could speak for as long as I needed to. I wasn't rushed. I was able to speak with God in the same way I would speak with Sean and Connor. It was awesome running down the long road knowing that He was all mine. He could hear my prayers. The morning after sleeping at Sand Mountain, however, I was having a less than favourable moment with God. To be honest I completely lost it. My feet were still badly blistered and very sore from the constant pounding they were taking. My niggling knee injury had flared up and I had managed to get sunburnt the previous day and movement made me wince in pain. In the constant overbearing heat, there was also some tension between me, Sean and Connor.

"God what have I done to you? Have I not suffered enough?" I screamed. I was scarily angry.

My pace was slowing as I made my way over my first set of mountain peaks and passes. Now, barely able to walk I took out my frustrations on the only person I knew would stick around to listen.

"I have given you everything I have got over the past six years, Father. I have become a better person; I have dedicated my life to help others. I put them before everything. My kids are suffering, my wife is suffering, all I ask is that you give me a break and give me the strength to complete my journey with less suffering. We have all suffered enough!"

I went on…

"I have sold my business, I have ignored my doctor's advice, I am financially ruined because I followed my calling. A calling that came from you. All the signs that guided me to this point came from you! For fuck's sake give me a chance to succeed!"

I ranted for about five minutes, although it felt longer. Eventually, I found myself resigned to the fact that I was on my own.

"OK Lord, as the saying goes 'thy will be done'; I trust you and love you. I know you will not abandon me."

I composed myself and, as it seemed to me, continued desperately shuffling up the next ridge.

About ten minutes later a man on a Harley Davidson pulled up alongside. This was not unusual. It was pretty common for drivers to pull up and make sure I was OK and occasionally call me crazy. This guy looked a little more concerned than usual. I do not know whether I was showing signs of distress, or what it was but he seemed genuinely concerned for my wellbeing.

"Hey man are you OK?" he asked in his awesome American accent.

"Ah, you know not bad, although I've had better days," was my less than convincing reply.

"Have you got water?"

"Yes."

"Have you got food?"

"Yes, I've got food."

"Have you got a place to stay tonight?" I was a little tired of his questions now.

"Yes, I've got a place to stay tonight." There was a short pause...

"Good, I am just making sure you have what you need," and with that he started his engine and rode off.

I was left stunned. Not because of the fact that someone had stopped but the way the conversation had ended. "I am just making sure you have what you *need*." He was right of course. How could I have not seen this earlier? I HAD everything I needed to succeed: water, food, shelter – OK, so I didn't have any luxury items but that is rarely the deal in life. God provides us what we need and not what we want.

I was left looking to the sky, marvelling at his great creation and how simple he had made it and laughing at how complicated I had made it. My mindset changed there and then. I finally accepted my situation and I was able to say with confidence that from then on I never felt truly alone.

From Sand Mountain our next stop was Middlegate – this now started to feel like the Wild West. A bar in the middle of the desert and our little oasis in the shape of a timber-framed building with a corrugated roof and a veranda and an old abandoned cart out front. This place was an original 100% piece of American history. Camping out the night before the food had been dire, I hoped that Middlegate would at least do a decent burger. They did not disappoint. We all tucked in to a big feed surrounded by all sorts of memorabilia from a bygone age: wanted posters and bulls' skulls, pictures of cowboys and guns. It was an awesome place to find in the middle of nowhere. They also had a motel attached to the bar. Now, when I say motel I mean a wooden shack with two beds shoved in, again, very basic but it was better than sleeping in a tent and it also meant I could get a much-needed shower. It felt so good to get all the sand out of my still painful toes.

I think we underappreciated these places. Looking back the effort and financial hardship on the owners of places like Middlegate must be immense. All just to provide fuel, food and shelter for a handful of people every week. I, for one, am very thankful now that places like this exist. I will never go past a remote restaurant or motel again without thinking of my time in Middlegate.

By this time, running for hours everyday through an epic, yet unrelenting landscape, it is hard to get across the isolation I was feeling Even during our stay in Middlegate the conversation was mainly between the three of us. Apart from a brief conversation with a couple who were cycling across America and the odd driver who stopped to see if I was crazy, I had hardly spoken to another soul since leaving Carson City. I am not a socialite by any stretch of the imagination but I do like to talk … lots. My kids are great for chitter chatter. It doesn't have to be deep and meaningful for me just a good chat about nothing keeps me happy. I wasn't getting any of this. I was even finding it hard to talk to Sean and Connor. I almost felt as though I was becoming a little bit crazy. All I had to stimulate my mind was long straight roads. Even listening to music didn't relieve my isolation. My chats with God certainly became longer and more profound at this stage, which meant I found Nevada to be a very spiritual place where I could really reach deep into my heart to find some answers. Stuff that I had not dealt with from my past was becoming an issue. People I had upset, I asked God for their forgiveness; work I had not done, I asked for another chance to complete; I often asked to be a better father. This last one is something I struggled with for long periods in Nevada and probably still do.

I had left my children at home whilst I ran off to America for four months. I remembered how I had felt when my father left to work in London for six months in the 1980s. I was devastated and I know it was at a significant point of my life. Sadly, for me, due to my dad's early death, I never got a chance to speak about those feelings. Knowing this I still did it to my own kids. I hope that I can speak to them about how they felt whilst I was away. I hope it doesn't scar them like it did me. Despite me saying I wouldn't become my father there are distinct similarities developing that I need to change. This was all going through my head as I battled mile after mile on the loneliest road.

The town of Austin was a welcome relief. A small town of less than 500 souls, there were a couple of motels, two restaurants and a bar – perfect! I had to rest up. Even though I had been hitting good daily mileage, despite my aching knee and sore feet, I knew that Sean and Connor needed a break too, so, for team morale we decided to have the day off.

I was sitting on the porch of our motel with my feet in a bucket of ice water, when we got chatting to two Canadians who were in the next room. I asked them what brought them to this part of America. "We are gold prospectors." Wow I wasn't ready for that answer!

"Aren't you 150 years too late lads?" was my immediate response, to which they laughed. It turned out they owned a mining operation and that despite the famous Gold Rush being long forgotten there actually was still lots of gold to be found in Nevada. You just have to own large mining equipment to get your hands on it. I find the search for gold fascinating and although the science behind it has changed the passion for the glittering metal hasn't. Just talking to the guys had me dreaming of finding a big gold nugget, sadly, I knew I stood more chance of a chicken nugget, but we can all dream!

These small towns are strange places when you are used to the big cities. People, although they rely on the tourist trade, seem a little reluctant to get to know you. This is probably explained best by an old lady who maintained that Austin is a pretty boring place to live: "We fish and we fuck," the sweet 80-year-old explained, "And in the winter there's no fishing." Apart from the people and the picture of a man hanging from a lamppost after a lynching, Austin itself was pretty nice. Sitting almost at the top of a mountain, the 360-degree views looking out over the great basin were spectacular. A seemingly unspoilt land with vibrant blue skies highlighting the rugged beauty of the mountain ranges, strangely, I was drawn to the one man-made bit that I found beautiful: the road east, Highway 50 winding its way over and through the mountains. Looking like it had been there forever, I cry as I write about it, that road, that single ribbon of tarmac laid by men just like me so many years ago would carry me east and to a new life. Our rest was perfectly timed, I thought as I looked towards the rising peaks of the next series of mountains – the next 200 miles of my journey.

Nevada's mountain passes are not a quick up and over like the ones I'm used to back home in Yorkshire. In this desert state the road rises relentlessly over a five-mile stretch before the last couple of miles over each summit. Sadly, the downhill run never seemed to last as long and I had 16 passes to negotiate. There is always something special about climbing a mountain or reaching a summit; regardless of how hard you find it, it still feels like an awesome accomplishment and I loved reaching the summit signs. They became my little motivators. Every time I reach the top I would spend ages trying to get my selfie with the sign behind me. It was a morale booster. Knowing that you have struggled and achieved anything in life gives you confidence to continue. By hitting these summits every day I felt I was achieving something special. I loved that feeling even if it did hurt like hell.

In one of the passes, as I ran towards the summit, another driver stopped. He was going in the opposite direction but, as the road was quiet, he did a three-point turn in his big RV and pulled up in front of me. Now, I always got a little nervous when a driver pulled up (the result of watching too many shows about American serial killers I imagine).

"Dude are you crazy?"

"Probably," was my response. I told the man and his wife what I was doing as they were astonished. They wished me well and presented me with two fresh red apples. Fruit! Wow, I hadn't seen fruit for weeks. "Thanks man," I said – I had already got into the American lingo! Boy that apple tasted good. I left Sean and Connor to fight over the other one. Fresh fruit in the desert tastes so gooooood!

Another night camping under the stars just off Hickison Summit allowed us time to talk as a team. We lit a fire and cooked a big pan of pasta and sat talking around the crackling flames. I was becoming increasingly annoyed at the lack of commitment from both Sean and Connor. Lately, they were acting like it was just a bit of a lads' holiday and I felt they had lost sight of how important the success of the trip was to me, my family and every addict that would hear of our journey. Checkpoint meets, timings, routes, arranging accommodation, things were slipping and not in my control when I was running. It felt like they had forgotten what was important, as I approached our car at several checkpoints that day it was almost as though they found me an inconvenience. They were reacting instead of being pro-active. I became quite emotional when I said the words, "If I fail at this I'm finished ... If I don't get to New York I will be a failure for the rest of my life," There was silence. "Lads, this is not a joke for me, I have given up everything to be here! This has to work. We all need to be on board otherwise we may as well just go home now." It needed to be said, as both Sean and Connor acknowledged they had let things slide. We needed to unite and I think on that evening we did.

Eureka was a place I wanted to visit just because, well, it's called Eureka! Sadly, the town didn't live up to its exciting name. Another one street town with sideways glances, although, I'll admit eating Chinese food in the middle of the desert was pretty cool. It was the best tasting food I'd had for weeks, unfortunately, my stomach did not agree. I may be being a little unfair to some of these towns. As I was simply passing through it may well have been my attitude towards the inhabitants, rather than theirs towards me, or it could simply be the dodgy running shorts I was wearing. Unshaven and exhausted, I did look a bit weird I suppose.

FB post 2 June 2013 Les Coleman
A lonely road maybe. But you are not alone Tom. A little (OK Big) bit of Wakefield is with you in spirit.

The roads stayed long and straight for most of the loneliest road and I did manage to zone out for long periods of the day, not because the landscape was any less spectacular, it was, but after a few days it became monotonous and rather boring. Luckily, I seem to cope quite well with boredom. Throughout my life, during long bouts of depression, I have spent many hours sitting inside looking at the same four walls. Even now, writing this book, I haven't been out of the house for two days but I'm still managing to remain sane. It's easy to say "I'm bored" and give up, it's quite tough to say "I'm bored ... So what?" I just lost myself in a world of cowboys and Indians and imagined the hardships suffered by those early pioneers. I had it pretty easy really.

Talking of cowboys, it was around this time that I saw my first real cowboy. From a distance I could see a truck and trailer pull over, two people disembarked two horses and rode off into the distance. I presumed the riders just decided to make the most of the wild country to give their horses a run out during a long journey. As I got closer I could see they were proper cowboys rounding up cattle. I couldn't believe my luck. I love the fact that people still do this for a living. This would be a great photo opportunity. I drew level with them just as they were corralling the final few cows into a truck. It was an older man and his daughter. He shouted to his daughter that he wanted to speak to the traveller and could she finish up on her own? He approached on his horse and asked me my story.

I told him the standard stuff that I was running across the States. Getting interested he dismounted and shook my hand with a really strong grip – just how I imagined a cowboy handshake to be...tough! We spoke for a few minutes and then he asked me a question out of the blue: "Do you have the Lord Jesus Christ in your life?" Wow, I thought, you'd never get asked that question in the UK!

"Yes I do," was my simple answer. He then went on to explain. His name was Jack and he was the Pastor of the local church. Again, I could not believe my good fortune that even in a desert I had found a man of faith. He spoke with me for about five minutes telling me his story – of mistakes in his early years and his subsequent change of lifestyle and devotion to Christ. He then did the most wonderful thing and asked if he could pray with me. You really have to picture the scene. In the middle of the loneliest road in America stand a cowboy and an ultra runner deep in prayer at the side of the road, lost in a moment of pure humanity and faith. He prayed that I would get to New York safely and that my message would be received everywhere I went. This is one of my favourite moments of the whole trip and one that still makes me feel good about life.

Progress on Highway 50 was slow going and oddly, I felt that I never really got myself into full running mode. Maybe I had just convinced myself that survival was my best and only option. To try anything else would be fool-hardy. A combination of the intense heat, seemingly endless roads and mountain passes made it difficult to set new challenges or be optimistic every day.

From Eureka to Ely I had four summits to climb. By this stage the loneliest road had got the better of me. I think Sean and Connor got a little concerned about my mental state. No matter how I felt on the road I always tried to put on a brave face at the checkpoint, but, I could no longer hide the fact that I was breaking down. As I saw the support car leave after a water stop my mood sank. Another summit called Robinson's Pass was in front of me. It was only five miles to the summit but it was a long slow drag. I saw a car pull up in the distance, the passenger door opened and someone got out. The car quickly then turned and shot off over the summit. "Who the hell is this?" I thought, squinting to see through the heat haze. It then clicked it was Connor! Sean had realised how low I'd been feeling and spoke to Connor to see if he would do the summit with me. Without hesitation Connor said yes.

Just to put this in perspective, Connor is only eighteen with no running experience. To volunteer to run in such hostile conditions to help a friend is outstanding. I smiled a big smile every mile up to the top of Robinsons', just having some company on the loneliest road was enough to see me through.

Although we still had some way to go before the state line we had now made it to the last official town in Nevada. Ely was a little bigger than the other towns we had passed through but it still had that air of mistrust. You could tell from the murals on the walls that this town had a very rich history. These streets had seen some action. A large mining town with lots of hotels and bars but also for the first time in almost three hundred miles some residential areas. Proper homes not trailer parks. It almost felt civilised.

The golden arches of McDonald's, heralded a big feed and boy it tasted so good! Being able to sit in a McDonald's doesn't sound that appealing in normal circumstances but these were not normal circumstances. Sitting in an air-conditioned restaurant with proper Wi-Fi to connect to the outside world was amazing. Our comms throughout Nevada had been poor with little or no phone signal and when we did find Wi-Fi it was so slow it wasn't worth the effort. I think that double quarter with cheese and the strawberry shake was the nicest I'd had since we left San Francisco, but food and McDonald's proved to be a bit of an undoing later in the trip.

Leaving Ely I knew I had accomplished something special. To have survived Highway 50 with little experience of what I was actually doing showed me that I have something or someone pushing me hard inside.

My determination to succeed was immense. I still had some way to go before I reached Border Town on the Utah state line but I was feeling proud of myself.

Sacramento was the final mountain pass, rising to 7,154ft above sea level. As I reached the summit I felt a range of emotions. I cried lots (not unusual for me!) but when I finally composed myself I recorded a video diary...

"Today is a big day. I am just getting out of Nevada. Something happened in Nevada that I can't explain and it's completely changed me. I suppose over time it will be revealed to be true but I feel completely different. I feel broken and rebuilt. An amazing experience, absolutely amazing. It's going to change some lives, Run4Sobriety, it's going to change some real lives."

Border Town was in the distance. I was ready for Utah and the rest of America. I was Battle Born.

CHAPTER 9

Utah

2,448.29 miles to go
New shoes and walking the line

Border Town gave me my first taste of the very different laws enforced by different states. Nevada has legalised gambling and casinos were a big part of the local economy. Utah doesn't allow gambling and also has restrictions on the sale of alcohol. With the state line dissecting Border Town they simply built the casino and bar on the Nevada side and the motel on the Utah side – simple really, allowing owners and punters to have the best of both worlds. Now, as none of us actually gambled or drank alcohol these attractions were lost on us, but what did attract us to the bar was the conversation.

A simple conversation between complete strangers became very important and could keep me occupied for at least an hour. We also played pool but all I wanted to do was take my coffee over to a table and listen to the chit-chat going on at the bar. It wasn't that interesting, it was just that I was so isolated during the daily run I was glad to hear new voices and get away from my inner monologue.

The stimulation of listening to people chatting combined with blue Powerade and 90s dance music made for a lively night in the motel; the relief of leaving Nevada combined with the sugar rush had me dancing around Sean's bed in my boxer shorts whilst singing 'Ebeneezer Goode' by the Shamen. I think Sean and Connor thought I had finally lost it – I hadn't, I was just feeling really good about our progress.

My elation, however, was to be short lived when the next day I saw a route sign for the town of Delta, which was 88 miles away. It seems the loneliest road may technically end in Nevada but in reality it continues in spirit for much further!

"I wonder why they call it Snake Valley?" I remember thinking to myself. It's one of those questions you are glad you don't say out loud as it's pretty dumb! "Because it's full of snakes, dickhead!" Within 30 minutes of leaving Border Town I had come across my first real live snake. That sudden, drenching cold rush of fear shot through my body. I don't like snakes. I have never been anywhere near them unless there was an inch-thick piece of glass and a lid keeping it in its tank at the zoo, and my anxiety, I think, goes back to my childhood.

In my local church there was a statue of the Virgin Mary holding the baby Jesus looking very much a gentle lady, yet when you look at her feet she is crushing a snake with her foot. The snake depicts the Devil, so from then on I always related snakes to evil or sin. Obviously, I am a little wiser and now and know that they are fairly gentle creatures but they still scare the shit out of me. Bearing this in mind I don't know where I got the courage from to take out my camera to photograph it and then, because I wasn't happy with the shot, I went in for a close-up! Talk about facing your fears.

Another new phenomenon was the difference in heat. Whilst the heat of Nevada felt like it was burning through you, running through Utah felt like having a hair dryer blowing in your face all day. Hot winds were certainly new to me. Where I come from when it's windy you're more than likely to freeze your balls off than work up a sweat. The heat was ridiculous and for the first time went over 40 degrees! I had visions of Sean and Connor being found dead, shrivelled and dehydrated inside the car. Thankfully, I didn't find them dead, I did, however, find them asleep. As I approached the car on one of my last checkpoint stops of the day I realised that Sean was sleeping. I got a little closer to see that Connor too was fast asleep. I love scaring people! This would be a great time to scare the shit out of these two! I crept closer to the car trying to stay as quiet as I could. I knew what was coming and nearly blew it by laughing. I approached the driver's window, which was open, and put my head as close to Sean's ear as I could. I paused... "WAKE UP MOTHERFUCKER! THIS IS A ROBBERY!" The expression on Sean's faced was priceless. "WWWWWAAAAAAAA!" he screamed as he drew his fist and punched me in the face, then whipping around to Connor, hit him as well, he then woke up and also screamed. As they were both trying to figure what had just happened I was literally rolling on the floor pissing myself with laughter! Due to the speed at which Sean shot off I don't think he saw the funny side of it!

These would be Connor's last few days on the trip. He had agreed to come for a month and to be honest he probably picked the toughest month of the three. He was immense – a constant source of both humour and annoyance. Sean and I would miss his company as the journey progressed.

The good thing about travelling across an entire country is that you see things that, otherwise, you would miss and, possibly, the country would prefer you'd missed too. Not that it's purposely hidden, it's just that they would rather it was left undiscovered. Just outside Delta is the Topaz Concentration Camp, which during World War II interned 110,000 people of Japanese ancestry. In the heat we were experiencing I have a fair idea of how those people suffered and it was another stark reminder of how easy I was really having it.

At this stage we were joined by my friend Catherine who we had collected from Salt Lake City and from where we released Connor back into normality. Whilst in Salt Lake City I was finally able to get some new trainers. Just being in the store made me feel so relieved. I tried on several pairs and realised that my feet had grown from a size 10 to 12.5. The constant impact on my poor feet had left me like Bigfoot! 'The Irish

Sasquatch' as Sean called me. I splashed out and bought three new pairs, hoping they would last me until I got over the Rocky Mountains, as I knew there would be no more stores until then.

Onward toward Provo and my first big city for some time. Running in new shoes was awesome and really did the trick. Even though my pace didn't improve much I was moving pain free for most of the day. Good shoes are of paramount importance, I had run almost 700 miles up to that point in complete agony. I now felt like I was floating on air.

Catherine hit the ground running, although probably didn't know what had hit her when we made camp for the night in Little Sahara. Yet another desert landscape, I think Catherine was surprised at how basic everything was. No shower or running water at this camp and constant noise from the local motocross gang. Still it was another beautiful place to stay. The sand dunes created a magical feel with thousands of stars shining above us. We could have been weary travellers in Egypt or Morocco. Sand and stars are a beautiful combination, as they almost reflect each other, millions of stars in the sky and millions of grains of sand. It was a mirror image. It was also very bloody cheap, so let's not get too philosophical here!

FB post 12 June 2013 Andrea Williamson
Tom – the other day you met a friend of mine who is cycling across the country and he's shared your website and FB page with a bunch of people who I'm sure are going to enjoy following your adventure. All of Bill's friends are sending you strong vibes as you continue your amazing journey!

Running in Utah I became more relaxed. I was now feeling much happier about my footwear and I was finally getting used to the heat (now hitting 30 degrees). Our daily routine was set and I pretty much knew what was ahead of me. We would wake around 6.30 a.m. and Sean would prepare breakfast or go and buy it depending on where we were staying. I would usually wait for as long as possible to get out of bed. Mostly I would eat breakfast whilst still in bed. This was usually a bacon and egg combo with lots of hash browns and pancakes if available and a lot of coffee was always needed to get both Sean and me going. I would start running at 9 a.m. taking a break every 4 or 5 miles with lunch at noon. I would keep the same pattern until I had hit my target of 30 miles or until I was 'cooked'. Having this regular routine definitely helped and we stuck to it as closely as possible. This pattern allowed me to get my head down and put in some good mileage.

Leaving Little Sahara we headed for another town called Eureka. This was not on the original route but it seemed to make more sense when I looked on the map. What I didn't notice on the map was the elevation. At 6500ft, it was a steep climb and, to be honest, even after a big carton of ice cream after 20-odd miles, I was pretty cooked by the time I got to the summit. I had done 30 miles and was almost finished when I saw a fantastic sight. The Uinta Mountains in the distance and a lovely big downhill section into the valley. How could I not want to carry on running? It was spectacular. I was surrounded by soaring peaks and a fast downhill switchback road with big sweeping curves, at the edge of which I could glimpse the beautiful state of Utah. The magnificence of the mountains and the inky dark blue sky as dusk drew in took my breath away. I was starting to understand how lucky I was to be able to run in such a wonderful landscape. As I hit my stride I was thankful for the cooling mountain air, it was fresh and clean. I took deep breaths as my body became re-energised. It felt like the air was filling my lungs with success, I was starting to believe in myself.

As I made my way to the bottom of the mountain I was gesturing to Sean and Catherine that I wanted to continue and I'm sure I caught a slight look of disbelief on their faces as I powered past them. Was this the same guy who struggled all day in the heat and was ready for quitting at the top of the mountain? I knew I was getting a little carried away but, to be honest, I loved being able to run this freely without limitations. The day finished at 6.40 p.m. having done 33 miles. I was happy.

Sean and Catherine had found a bed and breakfast place to stay, which was unusual and it did not really appeal to me. Too many dingy and rule-bound ones in the UK had scarred me for life and I figured the longer I stayed on the road the less time I'd have to stay at the grotty B&B. Boy was I wrong. The Tintic Goldminers' Inn was run by a lovely couple by the name of Margaret and Norman Gillen. It was a beautiful big old house set up in the hills and the rooms had lovely firm inviting beds. Sean had played an ace with this find.

Margaret made a lovely evening meal for us and, despite a slight embarrassing moment of eating before saying grace, sorry Margaret, we all tucked into our first home-cooked meal since leaving England over a month earlier. It was fantastic. I think I under-value the benefits of home-cooked meals. I really did feel like I was at home, I felt welcome. We sat around the table discussing everything from faith and politics to gold mining – Norman had a wealth of knowledge that I could listen to all night. Just as we were about to head off to bed, everyone was looking a little sleepy by this stage, there was a knock on the door. A young couple came in who knew the Gillens and had called in to see them. Tacoma and Tara introduced themselves and sat with us at the table. They chatted to us like we had been friends for a lifetime. They showed a genuine interest in what I was doing and really got behind the whole event. Both Tara and Tacoma had come into contact with addiction in their lives and really supported the need for us to speak out more. Also both are from New York so got pretty excited when I told them I was to finish in their home town. Meeting people like Tacoma and Tara, Norman and Margaret, really gave me a lift. Knowing that putting myself through all the pain and suffering actually meant something to someone was a super feeling. I feel truly blessed to have had this chance meeting and, thanks to Facebook, I still speak regularly with Tacoma and Tara. I really enjoyed my stay at the Goldminers' Inn. If you ever find yourself in Eureka, Utah be sure to pop in and say hello to Norman and Margaret.

Leaving their welcome was quite tough. It was Father's Day in the UK and both Sean and I had received cards from home and we really missed our kids. Mixing those feelings with the homely welcome we had received I think gave us both a heavy heart that morning.

However, the gorgeous scenery more than brightened our day – a picture postcard view, bright blue sky with snow-capped mountains for as far as the eye could see, although the temperatures were still in the 30s, it was almost perfect. I remember saying to Catherine, "How the hell did we end up in Wakefield?" I like living in Wakefield but this view blew me away. I was so jealous of the people who were fortunate enough to have this as a back drop every day. I hope they all appreciate how lucky they are.

Utah is also the home of the Mormons and I really did get a sense that life was lived a little bit closer to God around these parts than in Nevada. The state-controlled liquor laws appeared to have reduced the number of liquor stores and I got the impression that the Mormons would definitely frown upon drunkenness. This isn't to say that I'm naive enough to think that Utah doesn't have its alcohol problems, I just like the fact that in Utah I wasn't the odd one out for wanting to be sober. I thought that was pretty cool. The whole place just had a friendlier vibe going on.

Moving up through Spanish Fork the countryside over-flowed with cherry orchards and fields of livestock. There was finally something else to stimulate my mind apart from long straight roads, sand and rocks. Catherine usually joined me for a few miles each day, which was good. Sharing a view is so much better than marvelling at it alone, no matter how amazing.

Staying over at a motel in Provo next, it was evident that, although the alcohol seems to be controlled the drugs are definitely not. The hotel had some colourful characters hanging around and although we didn't feel threatened I think Catherine was a little nervous of our surroundings. We would eventually get used to the cheap motel clientele – to be honest I think we became the cheap motel clientele as the weeks went by.

Running east, I was super excited to be heading up into the mountains again. I knew that even though it was going to be tough the rewards would be great. The only difficulty I faced was the traffic and this was scary shit. A two lane concrete highway took me out of Provo up through Provo Canyon. The traffic speed was ridiculous and the noise was driving me crazy, so much so we bought ear plugs to help block it out. Nevada had been kind to me really. The traffic count was low and the drivers were always courteous, often waving or pipping their horn. These guys were different. Pedestrians were like aliens, they don't exist. I just tried my best to blank out the noise and push on. The good thing was that the hard shoulder was plenty big enough to leave space between me and the trucks. This was the first time it occurred to me that if a driver makes one mistake I'd be dead. I quickly had to put that thought to the back of my mind.

I was now running through the most spectacular mountain ranges I had ever seen. Heading toward them since leaving Eureka, I was now actually up close and personal with the rock. Towering above the canyon road was Mount Timpanogos which rises up over 12,000ft, 5,000ft of which appeared to be looming right over me. Being surrounded by mountains like this was yet another first for me. I have never been in mountains of this size before. It made me feel very insignificant, I can certainly see why the Native American Indians give them so much respect. The rock has such a great physical presence, it's almost like it's alive and there was a spot, a particular place that we took time out to explore.

Bridal Falls is an awesome 600-foot high waterfall. Sean had called me to say he'd pulled off the road to take a look. When I got there I could see why. It was stunning. Apparently, legend has it that a young Native American Indian girl jumped off the cliff edge after her lover had been killed, after which the water started to flow as Mother Nature felt the girl's sorrow. Whatever the story, it was a wonderful place to visit and take a few pictures.

Alongside Highway 189 runs the Provo River. As I moved higher through the canyon the river started to widen out and I could imagine in the spring after the winter thaw the river would be a fantastic sight

– roaring and tumbling between the rocks. Today, it was much more genial. In the distance I could see some fishermen standing in the middle of the river. As I got closer I could see that it was a father and his son. The image was perfect. So much so, that I took a photograph. When you have been away from your children for a long time you begin to think hard about your parenting skills. Here this man was spending quality time with his son, whilst I was 5,000 miles away from mine. I just wanted to be that man for an hour or so. Before I left home spending 'man time' with Oliver had become quite a regular thing. Making that time to bond father to son I think gave him the confidence to allow me to go away for so long. He knew I would be back. He knew his dad would not let him down. Saying that, it still hurt like hell seeing any dad on the trip having time with their kids.

As I moved up to Deer Creek Reservoir the views just kept getting better. Although I was completely shattered by the time a cyclist flew past me almost at the top of the last climb, it was worth it. I can't say enough times or really be able to describe just how beautiful Utah was – it was simply the most beautiful landscape I had ever seen in my life.

Heber City was not what I would call a city although it did have all the usual fast food establishments (I'm sure that that's all it takes to make a town into a city in the States, "Do you have a McDonald's? Yes, then you are a city, congratulations!") And it was here that Sean decided it was time to have his hair cut; not much to write home about really ... unless you have your hair cut by Dick!!

Heber City Dick had just recovered from open-heart surgery and clearly was not a well man. His hands were shaking whilst he held the blunt scissors. He realised Sean was from England and told him how he loved British comedy. Well that was it as far as Sean was concerned. He was having a good conversation about one of favourite TV programmes, 'Dad's Army' and forgot that Sweeney Todd appeared to be about to cut his hair. He kept his faith in the man and went ahead with the cut! Needless to say afterwards Sean looked like he'd had surgery himself.

"Hey Sean, did you get your hair cut by Dick?" was the standard 'let's piss Sean off' quote for the rest of the trip.

My biggest climb to this point was along Highway 40 up to Daniels Summit. Topping out at just over 8,000 feet, the road was one of the main routes linking the West Coast with Denver and the traffic was becoming more hazardous. This meant that volume and speed would increase and, sadly, the hard shoulder would decrease. It was time to start walking the line.

The solid white line that marked the road from the hard shoulder was my only protection between life and certain death. At this stage of the run I was running with the traffic. I had a theory that if I was going to be hit I didn't want to see it coming, I did, however, change this approach later in the trip. In order to tackle this sort of journey you have to be realistic. There were always going to be drivers who took the corner too tight or drivers that would look at the map or even be sending a text. I just had to be on my guard at all times. I was super alert during the first section coming out of Heber City. The increase of semis (a combination of a huge truck towing a big trailer) was alarming. They didn't hold back either! When they hit the bottom of the hill there would have to be an apocalyptic event to stop their progress. I suppose that's their game. Hauling ass over the mountains! I never got in the way of a semi. I could usually hear them coming and would allow lots of room for them to pass. Most of them tried to leave me enough room but one or two got rather too close for comfort.

As I got higher the temperature lowered, although it would still be considered a hot summer's day in the UK at 29 degrees, but I was now getting used to it and the cooling breeze off the mountains was certainly welcome. I could also feel the air getting thinner. My throat was becoming very dry and at times I was struggling to catch my breath. Although we're not talking about the dizzying heights of the Himalayas I did notice a real difference. My body found it more of a struggle – I don't know all the technical stuff but I do know that it made an already tough climb even harder. The night was drawing in on us as we approached the summit. Catherine had joined me for the last section and we were treated to a family of deer crossing the highway, a magical sight. Everything was so still as the deer approached and, with hardly a sound, they were over the road, leaping away through the beautiful mountain meadows. Wild animals are truly fantastic in their own environment, it's like they just flow with their surroundings. We reached the summit at sun down, which seemed like perfect timing. I loved my time in the mountains, for some reason I felt at home.

The landscape after Daniels Summit took on a different look and feel, it was like a mountain desert – vast swathes of scrub land and, if I'm honest, a little disappointing. I had expected the land and views this high up to be forest and grass lands, but sadly not, just lots of dust and very strong winds! The only sights of any real beauty were the reservoirs. Strawberry and Starvation Reservoirs were lovely rugged bodies of water that looked part of the natural surroundings and we were fortunate enough to spend a couple of nights camping beside Starvation Reservoir – a beautiful location to hide away from the traffic and the heat of the day.

As we clocked up the miles on this stretch, the traffic was getting ridiculous. The oil industry features heavily in the area and, as such, the amount of semis increased dramatically. Up until this point I had run with the traffic, as I would rather not see what was about to kill me. Catherine, on the other hand, had repeatedly pleaded with me to reconsider and, with the sudden increase of traffic I decided that I would swap sides if I thought my life was in more danger than it was already. Running down into the town of Vernal that moment came.

After a comfortable night's sleep in a log cabin at Starvation Reservoir I was feeling fresh. The facilities were fantastic. I had managed to get a great shower and was on good form and the previous day had seen me make great progress towards the town of Vernal. I had also noticed a slight increase in the volume of trucks but was not that concerned. Today, was to be very different. The semis seemed to be on their own today. They outnumbered the cars two to one. Their speed had increased also. Catherine decided not to join me for her usual four miles, she felt that it was too dangerous to be driving on the road let alone running on it. Undeterred, I got my head down and got on with it. Closer and closer the trucks came to hitting me. The road had plenty of bends and to negotiate the curves these guys were using the entire road, including the hard shoulder, and it didn't seem to occur to them to use their brakes. I kept going and tried to ignore the problem, yet I flinched every time I heard behind me the deafening noise of truck tyres hitting the rumble strip. Was this it? Was I going to be hit?

At every checkpoint I laughed it off saying it was fine and that I was enjoying the battle. I suppose I was in a way but the constant anxiety and tension was beginning to get to me. By this stage I was wearing ear defenders, so I could cut out the noise. I could still hear things but they allowed me to be able at least to hear my own thoughts.

I remember praying hard after lunch that day, as I knew it must only be a matter of time before something hit me. I asked to be kept safe and to be guided through the rest of the day. At around 3 p.m. I had had enough. I needed to get off the highway. We headed straight for the motel. My breathing was a little erratic and as I reached my room my whole body gave up on me. I fell on the bed and started to cry, my body convulsing. Sean started to panic. I heard him asking what was wrong. I thought I was having a heart attack. He thought I was having a heart attack. I lost consciousness for a minute or so, but when I came round I felt calm. I felt safe again. Sean looked pale and worried. I was fine. I had got myself so worked up I think I had a panic attack, that was all I assured him. Deep down I don't know what happened that day. I guess I'll never know.

I still had to get back out on the road that evening to complete the day's mileage. We went for something to eat but all I could do was cry. Every time I went to speak nothing came out, just more tears. It felt like

I had been broken. After all this time on the road had I finally lost the plot? How the hell was I going to continue? Was this the time to call it off, to go home?

Was it fuck!

As an addict you are going to have bad days. You are always going to have days where you think you have lost the plot that you have finally cracked. You have two options. The first, you go back to alcohol or drugs and hide away forever or, second, you dust yourself down suck it up and get back in the fight. I needed to suck it up and get back in the fight!

So at 6 p.m. I hit the road again. This time I ran facing the traffic. I put my favourite music on and enjoyed the last part of the day. As I came towards the final checkpoint Sean and Catherine could see me dancing along the highway singing D:Ream's 'Things can only get better' at the top of my voice. I had faced my fear and rather than letting fear win, I adapted to its challenge. I was not going to be beaten by the traffic or anything else that America had to throw at me. Every day I fight, every day I win!

CHAPTER 10
Colorado

2,091.79 miles to go
The goat, the seagull and a moose

Colorado was such an exciting state to reach. I think most people on the planet have heard of the Rocky Mountains. This vast mountain range is known as 'the Great Divide', as it cuts the entire continent in two. To have the opportunity to run across the Rockies was something I had never thought possible. 'Welcome to Colorful Colorado' read the sign! How could you not get excited about that? Sadly, that was about as exciting as it got for a few days.

Whilst organising the trip Orla and Oliver became enthusiastic at the prospect of me visiting the town of Dinosaur. Isn't it every child's dream to live in a place called Dinosaur? It was the first town over the state line and their infectious excitement had ensured that I couldn't wait to see what the town had to offer. Unfortunately, Dinosaur had nothing to offer but its name. A tired-looking town consisting of trailer parks and an information centre, there were no motels or restaurants, never mind a dinosaur, although, by the look of some of the ancient trailers I could have been mistaken. I was bloody annoyed! How can you have the best name in the world and not turn it into a kick-ass place to be? It was dire and to make matters worse there was no place to stay for at least another 60 miles. This would mean we had to drive back to Vernal for accommodation. I hated this, as it meant a long drive at night and then again in the morning before resuming the run, too much stress during an already stressful period.

By this stage I was struggling to eat. The constant anxiety of heavy traffic piled on top of simmering financial worries had me in a pretty bad place. I was also struggling to sleep. Ask anyone about endurance events and they will tell you that the most important things are sleep and nutrition and I wasn't doing either properly! I managed to Skype a good friend Andy McMenemy to discuss the situation. I respect very few people's opinions when it comes to advice about running. I find most people just give answers that they have read in a book or have heard another runner say. I needed to take advice from someone who knew what I was going through. Andy is one of those guys. In 2011 he completed 66 ultra-marathons in 66 days around 66 cities in the UK. It was a monumental effort. His body went through so much that he now has a wealth of knowledge about what takes to succeed and I knew he could help me.

"Eat the things you like, Tom, anything, don't worry about what it is, just get calories in. Just keep eating." This was music to my ears. Even though I was struggling with some foods I was able to eat ice cream and milk shakes. So that's what I did, whenever possible I had an ice cream or a milk shake. If that wasn't available I loved to eat skittles and M&Ms. Now this wouldn't solve my long-term eating problems but it would act as a bridge until I got my appetite back. The sleep issue would be something I would eventually get used to. I rarely slept well throughout the entire trip. Different motels and situations left my mind very active. Sleep would be less frequent visitor as the weeks went on.

As Colorado is mainly known for the Rockies I expected to be in the mountains as soon as I hit the state line. I had to wait. The first few days would be spent crossing wild landscapes that actually reminded me of the moorlands we have in the UK – just a lot drier and dustier. The dust got everywhere and filled my sinuses, so much so that I ended up with a pretty bad nosebleed. These were the lands you recognised from the cowboy movies when the hero rides off into the distance. In fact I would often lose myself thinking about days of the first pioneers. I would think of what it must have been like to be out on these lands trying to carve out a new life. Not knowing what lay ahead or what the future may hold. I drew strength from their spirit. I knew that if the early pioneers could survive then so could I. Looking over vast landscapes was not new, by this stage I had completed 1,000 miles of my 3,000 mile journey, but picking up my eyes up from the tarmac and looking out always reminded me how great the world is and also how great the world will continue to be long after we are all gone.

Maybell was the first place we found for 60 miles that had supplies. It also had a campsite and what looked like a hotel. Given the choice I would always prefer a hotel. So after a 36-mile day we drove the short distance to the hotel, which was directly opposite the campsite. The Old Victory Motel was a little bit run down. To be honest I was almost praying for it to be closed or full. It looked dodgy as hell. Sean and Catherine went to the front door and knocked. Nothing. They waited a few minutes and knocked again this time they could hear someone slowly making their way to the door. They could hear them fumbling about with keys trying to unlock the door. They then dropped the keys on the floor made a grunting noise and walked away. Sean and Catherine stood there politely expecting them to return with another set of keys. They didn't return, in fact Sean looked through the front window and saw an old man, who have evidently returned to the comfort of his arm chair. What a git! How the hell can you run a hotel like that? I was secretly pleased; even though I disliked camping I prefer it to sleeping in a psycho's house!

We pitched up and had a great feed of pasta! We didn't chat that much as we were all pretty exhausted and we were being eaten alive by mosquitos. The place was alive with them. There were so many a man drove around the village spraying chemicals to keep them under control. It wasn't working. We went to sleep safe in the knowledge that we would be bitten to death as we slept. Sure enough I woke to find I had been bitten on the arse seven times as well as having my forehead attacked. It was a pretty uncomfortable night.

The first big town we came to in Colorado was Craig, which was also going to be Catherine's final stop on our journey. Her two weeks had flown by. She was a great addition to the team and brought some good ideas for the rest of the trip. Again, I am grateful that she gave up her time to help me succeed. As a treat she took Sean and I out for a big meal at the Holiday Inn. This was definitely a luxury, as we were struggling financially. It was the first time we had sat down to a decent meal since Eureka in Utah. The waitress was a lovely lady who was very interested in what we were doing. She asked for my name so that she could pray for me. I loved this. Knowing that someone is prepared to take time out of their busy lives to pray for you is an awesome feeling. As we sat chatting to other people in the restaurant she brought out a huge piece of cake as a gift from her and the other waitress – such a lovely gesture.

Sean had to drive Catherine to Denver for her flight, we should have been further down the road than Craig but we were behind schedule, which meant he had a five-hour drive to get her there. I had originally planned to go with them but the thought of spending ten hours driving to and from Denver was not appealing. I decided to bed down in the hotel for a food and 'NCIS' TV marathon. Boy, was I ready for a break. The temperature had been really hot over the previous days hitting 37 degrees, so, to be able to get out of the sun for a day was bliss. Again, to outsiders this must have looked pretty strange. Checking into a motel and not moving from the room all day but it seriously was bliss. I ate as much food as I could then slept a little then ate some more then slept some more. Watched a little TV and, you guessed it, slept some more. It was just what I needed.

I was a little concerned for Sean and his journey to Denver. It was a difficult drive over the mountains. Yet again, we had no phone reception so I just had to wait for him to arrive back at the motel. I expected him back about nine p.m. but he arrived back at seven absolutely brimming with enthusiasm, "It's breath-taking, it's fucking awesome! I have never seen anything like it. The Rockies are going to kick our ass but it's going to be worth it!!" It had been a long time since I had seen Sean this excited. I knew seeing Colorado would open his mind to how fantastic this trip was. We had endured to this point, now we would be able to enjoy the ride for a few weeks. He was so excited we treated ourselves to a posh Wendy Burger – way over our meagre budget but the moment deserved it.

Whilst in Craig we heard about Steve Wescott. Steve is from Seattle and was walking across the USA with Leroy. Nothing strange you think, until you discover that Leroy is a goat. Yes, Steve is walking across the USA with a goat – I got my brother, Steve got a goat. Sean managed to spot him whilst driving to Denver and introduced himself. Steve was only about 20 miles further up the road, which meant I would catch up with him pretty quickly. To be able to chat to someone who was doing the same thing as me was awesome. I looked forward to finding out how he was managing to keep positive. He sent me a message to say he had left me a power bar at mile marker 117 on the highway, so I instantly knew he had a sense of humour. Sure enough at mile marker 117, slightly melted in the midday sun, I found a power bar gaffer taped to the post. I couldn't wait to catch up with this guy, especially after the morning I'd had...

Before I managed to get out of Craig I had to negotiate a couple of awkward junctions and shopping mall entrances. One of the strange rules of the road in the US is that you can turn right at traffic lights even when the signal is red, as long as it is safe to do so. Now that last bit, 'safe to do so' appears to be lost on many drivers. As I approached the crossing there was a woman sitting at the lights. I had the pedestrian walk light so I started to make my way across the junction. Suddenly I heard the revs of a car engine and looked up to see the woman in the stationary car was no longer stationary – she was, in fact, speeding towards me. All I could do was hop onto the car bonnet (à la Starsky and Hutch) and roll off the other side. I landed on my feet and instantly made my way towards her. "I didn't see you…" she protested weakly. "You didn't see me? I am six feet tall with a white t-shirt, a beard, a bandana and you didn't see me? Lady you need an eye exam!" She apologised and I accepted. No harm, no foul as they say.

Steamboat Springs is where the fun starts in the Rockies. Approaching the place I got a thrill of excitement. Running in a beautiful environment was exactly what I needed. With the mountains in the distance and tracking the Yampa River, it certainly was a beautiful place to run. Watching holiday makers drift down the river in a rich variety of inflatables made me very jealous; families out enjoying the day, mums and dads, brothers and sisters, I had to keep reminding myself I was not on holiday, I was working.

The town of Steamboat Springs is a very affluent area. The streets are so clean, I could have eaten off them – the shops and restaurants were certainly out of our price range. In the distance I could see a crowd gathering, all converging around one man. As I got closer I realised it was the 'goat man'! "Hey Steve!" I shouted across the street, "Dude, how's it going?" was his beaming response. Steve was super enthusiastic about what I was doing, but he was the only one. Everyone else wanted to know about his travelling companion, Leroy the Goat! Yes folks, I had run over a thousand miles to be upstaged by a goat. To be fair, what Steve had undertaken was a monumental task. Not only was he responsible for keeping himself safe but he was also responsible for the safety of Leroy. He had the added issue that everyone wanted a picture with him and the goat. This would slow him down to three miles per day at times and he was in his second year on the road having travelled just over one thousand miles. I admired his patience. I am not going to tell you Steve's story, as it is his to tell. What I will say is that we went for a meal where his mum Theresa joined us and we chatted for about two hours. His mother also had a great a journey to share as she was heading to Africa on mission work. It was a blessed evening and one I look back on with great fondness. The chances of meeting on this long stretch of road were slim, and I am thankful to God that He allowed our paths to cross.

The campsite Sean had managed to find was full, so they had given us a pitch on the overspill site. Wow, how cool was this campsite? The pitch was directly beside the Yampa River and I was able to soak my feet in cool, sparkling river water whilst drinking a double shot Americano from Starbucks (that's how posh this place was, they had a Starbucks!). It was a super place to relax after a perfect day on the road. That night we were treated to a fantastic electrical storm. I went to bed happy. Colorado was going to be a great state.

I was on the road early next day, facing my first big climb in the Rockies. Rabbit Ears Pass was a significant summit rising to 9,426 feet. It also marked the line of the Continental Divide. Although mileage-wise I wasn't half way this was a great milestone. The climb was brutal. From Steamboat to the top of the first of the Rabbit Ears was about seven miles and a climb of about 3,000 feet. It was bloody steep. There were a couple of cyclists coming downhill who were flying past me at breakneck speed. How I would love to go back and tackle the climb on a bike just for the downhill freewheel! One of them stopped to chat and told me that the climb to the top is worth it. "It was already worth it," I said, as I looked around at what I can only describe as Austria in the summer. Ski lodges dotted the lush green hillsides, as this was a prime ski resort in the winter but in the summer it was just as stunning. The high Rocky Mountains and the flat valley floor with river meandering through the picturesque town. He agreed and told me that his wife had come to Steamboat on holiday and fell in love with the place. They sold up and moved there the next month. It was funny, as I'd tried earlier to call Zoë to see if she could check out property prices in the area. It was the first place I had visited that I would have happily moved to.

The altitude I had been operating at was averaging at 6,000 feet up to this point. Previously I had run at 8,000 feet and I hadn't really noticed much difference in my performance apart from a sore throat and the odd headache. To head up to 9,500 feet was going to make quite a bit of difference. I was noticing that my throat was becoming quite dry and irritated and I started to struggle with my breathing. It was as though I had never run before. Once up on top of the first Rabbit Ear I had a short section before the next and that allowed me a brief respite from the climb; however, this short relief was rudely interrupted by a sudden downpour of rain.

I had experienced very little wet weather up to this point in the journey. What I was soon to learn was that, like everything in the States, when it rains it really rains! I got absolutely soaked in about two minutes. I ducked off the road and went into the forest to hide under a tree until Sean came back for me. I had gone from being pretty upbeat to being a moaning git in five minutes. Being wet when you are out on a mountain can be quite uncomfortable. I was cold; I hadn't been cold since I climbed Echo Pass five weeks earlier. It felt miserable. I sat in the car bemoaning my situation. I had no right to moan, I had had great weather to this point. It showed me how fragile my mood was. I had to be careful not to let my negative thoughts gain too much power over me.

After 30 minutes warming up in the car I set off again, still feeling quite sorry for myself. I saw a car pull over and three men got out. The older gentleman approached me and embraced me without saying a word. He then introduced his two sons and said he loved what I was doing and wanted to say a prayer with his sons and me. We stood at the side of the road in a huddle whilst this man blessed my journey with prayer. He shook my hand and he was gone! This random act of kindness really shook me up. I was beginning to realise that what we were doing was special. That we were on a special journey and when times got rough someone or something would always appear for me to lift me through the darkness.

I managed to continue the day up past the sign for the Continental Divide. This was pretty cool, as it was the first sign I had seen that mentioned the Atlantic waiting for me over 2,000 miles away along with New York. Sadly, the day had taken its toll. I had started to feel quite tired, not the usual fatigue, I was actually falling asleep whilst running. It is the same feeling you get if you are driving late at night were your head starts to nod. I think a combination of altitude, being soaked and then warming up quickly added to 42 days on the road meant my body had had enough. It needed to sleep. So, we stopped at a campsite at the top of Rabbit Ears Pass and got some well-earned food and rest and I deserved it! It's not every day you climb a 9,400 foot mountain.

My original route was taking me directly into Denver along Highway 40. Sean had driven the route a few days earlier, when he dropped Catherine at the airport and he was worried. He believed it would be very tough to negotiate the traffic system in Denver. There was also a tunnel with no pedestrian access. It was decision time. After a few days of going over options with route planner Zoë, I had to make up my mind. Do I continue on the Highway 40 and risk having to drive a section of the route or take a left on to Highway 14 and head towards Walden. Mileage-wise there wasn't much in it, in fact going through Walden would actually save me ten miles. It was the fact that we had made no plans to be up there. We had no idea of how remote it would be or how tough the route would be. At least with the Highway 40 I knew what I was getting. I knew there would be some killer mountains to climb and plenty of accommodation. The Highway 14 was the unknown. But, I always like to follow my heart and it was screaming "Highway 14!" so, I followed my heart. When you make a decision like that you almost always doubt it instantly but on this occasion I had no doubt this was the right way to go. It would get me away from the heavy traffic for a few days at the very least.

As I made my way up the first few miles of the highway I noticed that I was being followed by a seagull. Now, I know nothing about birds but I know a seagull when I see one and this one was a long way from home! As I ran along I began to wonder if this was some sort of a sign.

This single seagull was flying with me almost confirming that I had made the right decision. Taking this route would get me safely to the Atlantic. The seagull followed me for at least three miles and as quickly as it had appeared it was gone. I am sure some ornithologist will tell me that it is normal to have seagulls this far inland but I quite like my theory. I was being guided home.

The road was a welcome break from the constant battle on Highway 40. Although it wasn't completely quiet the road was one less travelled. I even managed to see a group of cowboys hard at work herding cattle. I find it amazing that herding cattle in these parts hasn't changed since the pioneer days. Some traditions should never be lost. I suppose it's still quite an effective way to farm on such vast open areas of pasture. Either that or the men just like dressing up and riding around!

After the constant roar of traffic I was happy with the new found solitude and silence. I had had a month of tough roads, so I was going to enjoy some peace and quiet. Well I was until a man jumped out from the bushes! Yes, out of nowhere a man appeared and was walking towards me. It turned out he was a Canadian called Sean who was walking the Continental Divide from Mexico to Canada – hard-core stuff! Sean was doing his trip unsupported and had a super attitude. He told me he had dreamed of doing this walk since he was a boy. Until I was planning my trip I hadn't even heard of the Continental Divide let alone dreamt of walking it! I have immense respect for people like Sean. He had a dream and he followed it through. I hope he managed to finish, I am sure he did.

Running in this area reminded me of home, not Yorkshire, but where I grew up in Ireland. What a ridiculous comment, Tom! How the hell can running in Colorado remind you of Ireland? I am serious, if you take away the bright blue sky and the heat, erase the backdrop of the Rocky Mountains and there you go: Ireland. Lush green land with cattle everywhere, lovely farm houses scattered across a landscape of rolling hills and the occasional tractor. It really did give me a feeling of home. For a time I just imagined I was home, running through the lanes near my mother's home village of Arvalee in County Tyrone. Memories and a wonderful sense of freedom came flooding back, out in the lanes riding my cousin Angus's racing bike out for hours on end. We were always sent down to Tyrone in the summer holidays. I loved it there away from all the bullshit at home and the troubles in Belfast. There was still sectarian tension in Tyrone but somehow it just felt easier to handle. I would ride further each day until I was confident I knew how to get home. Though there were times when I did wonder how far I could get before anyone would miss me. I felt that little of myself that I never tried, I thought that they probably wouldn't come looking, so what was the point? The ability to be able to lose myself for a few hours really helped during the journey. I was able to process so much of my life during these times, I often want to go back to Walden simply for the solitude.

The town of Walden was pretty similar to most of the towns we visited; just one main street with a couple of motels or restaurants and bars. I quite liked the place. It had a friendly vibe. The motel was great as we actually had two separate bedrooms. Sean and I had slept in the same room now for 43 days, privacy and space was very much valued.

Small towns like Walden don't have the luxury of take-away food so we had to scrub up before dinner. Our supper was served at a steakhouse that was full of very happy diners, we caught the mood and decided to treat ourselves to a big feed. Although we couldn't afford steak we could afford a big chilli burger with fries and onion rings! It was spectacular. My appetite had returned with a vengeance! Thankfully I was finally enjoying my food. Sean is not such a big eater. This started to annoy me a little when we went out for food and he left something on his plate. It didn't bother me so much when we ate at McDonald's, as it only cost a few bucks but in a restaurant it pissed me off. When we paid more for food I wanted it to be eaten. This was a principle lost on Sean. Sitting in a very busy restaurant I started to have a go at him about leaving some food on his plate. I was quite discreet but he heard me loud and clear. "For fuck's sake..." was his reply, "it's like eating my dinner with fucking

Top: Marathon Des Sables 2010

Left: Official start point for Run4Sobriety

Moving East
The lonliest road, Highway 50

Left: Sean and Connor — sand mountain

The cowboy preacher

Hot and hairy

Support staff
Catherine
in Utah

Steve and Leeroy the Goat

Highest point of the journey Climbing the Rockies

Bearded selfies

Surprise
support crew
Marty Acosta

Irish sunburn,
posh dinner
Holiday Inn
Quincy, Illinois

Bridge geek heaven

A bit of a boost to the run

Good friends
to finish

Hitler!" He had said this a little louder than I think he wanted to. We started to get evil stares from the table beside us, I thought we had upset them with our bad language. The waitress arrived at their table to start taking their order. We then realised why they had been offended. "I vould like zi booger wis ze fries und a side order of ze onion rings." What are the chances of being seated next to two German motor bikers in a Colorado restaurant? What are the chances of making a reference about Hitler whilst being sat next to two German motor bikers in a Colorado restaurant? It was time to get out of there before we ended up as part of their side dishes. Trouble was I couldn't move for laughing. The colour had drained from Sean's face and was getting more edgy by the second. It kind of felt like Karma for not eating his food. There was no mention of Hitler for the rest of the trip.

I was nearing the half-way point around this stage. Physically I was about to have one of my toughest days. As I left Walden I felt really good. We had eaten and slept well but I was aware that my legs had no power left. I have heard people say this before that their legs feel 'empty' but this was a little more than that – my entire body felt empty. Normally, after five or so miles I start to get into some sort of a rhythm but today there was nothing happening. As the day progressed I was getting slower and slower. It wasn't the hottest day I had endured but it was still over 30 degrees and I had a horrible feeling that today was the day I would fall to pieces. What scared me most was how quickly I had become fatigued. One day I felt fine and then the next, boom! I was exhausted. In situations like this it is extremely important that you try to understand what has happened. I went over in my head the previous few days and decided that I was probably still suffering from my climb over Rabbit Ears Pass. It was the only rational explanation. I needed to allow myself to believe this; I couldn't afford to let myself think I was finished.

The need to listen to music had diminished since hitting Steamboat Springs. The beauty of the place was entertaining enough; today I needed all the help I could get. I tried to listen to the 'Talk Ultra' podcast but that just made me feel like a complete failure. The show was full of reports of runners running hundred milers in 18 hours and that pissed me off. I was struggling to do three miles per hour! I decided to get some uplifting church music going. My church's band is called 'I Am Future' and I had their album on my phone. I listened to it from start to finish, just letting the words wash over me and allowing it to get through the day. It worked, arriving just outside Gould I had managed to do a good 27 miles and decided that was enough. As soon as the music finished I started to feel empty again and poor Sean copped for another barrage of abuse. My frustration around the day's struggles spilled out in pure anger. He did the right thing and disappeared for an hour to make dinner and to let me cool down. I went to sleep for an hour and then recorded a short video piece.

"Just finished day 44, it's probably the darkest day I have had so far. I don't know why, the scenery has been beautiful but there is just nothing in my legs; head's empty. I just really struggled today, I just wanted to go home but we kept fighting and managed to do 27 miles and got to a place called Gould. We now have Cameron Pass tomorrow so I'm going to get a big feed and an early night and hopefully I will feel better in the morning. It's the first time in 44 days I can honestly say I want to go home."

Looking back on that video I remember how dejected I felt. I really did feel defeated.

Of course I wasn't and after taking on some fluids and another feed of pasta, I started to brighten up. Sean and I discussed the day whilst watching yet another beautiful sunset. All we knew was that tomorrow was another day and we would be ready for it.

As it happened I did feel loads better the next day and although I wasn't super positive I was a little happier about what lay ahead. This is how my video diary sounded at the start of the day.

"Day 45 of Run4Sobriety. After yesterday's meltdown, and it was a complete meltdown, I lost it with Sean, I lost it with myself, but I've woken up this morning in a better mood.

I've just said a prayer asking Jesus for a bit more strength. I'm questioning why he has chosen me for this journey, there are times I question him because I don't think I'm strong enough for him to have chosen me, but you've got to keep your faith and that's what its all about, I keep on plodding on.

Quite an emotional day today because we are going over Cameron Pass and that's it for the Rockies it's downhill after that. I would imagine today is going to be fairly emotional because I hate the Rockies at the moment. I just want to get out of here. I love the scenery; I love everything else about it I just want to get out of the Rockies and onto the flats and start going home. Speak to you soon."

Even though I wasn't on a high I had managed to almost understand my role in all this, that I must keep the faith.

I got my reward going up Cameron Pass. It felt like sensory overload: mountains, deer, trees, bird song and bright coloured flowers all combined to renew my spirit and made for a wonderful day on the road. Since I arrived in Walden a few days earlier I had spotted warning signs for moose in the area. Walden's village sign proudly boasts 'The moose viewing capital of Colorado', naturally I had been slightly disappointed to find that they were not as easy to spot as first suggested. I hadn't seen a thing. Coming out of Gould I passed a farmhouse and standing next to some trees was what looked like a moose. It was huge! It was also very still. It's a statue I thought, there had been so many houses along the highway with deer statues in their front garden that I thought this must be the same thing. A very big, well carved, life-like statue of a moose. I didn't want to be just another tourist taking a picture of the wooden moose; I hated the thought of looking silly photographing a statue. So I put my camera away. As I walked passed this magnificent 'statue' it casually swung its head round to consider my progress. I jumped a mile – for fuck sake it's bloody real! But by the time I got the camera out it was gone. Sean didn't believe me when I rang him to tell him. No photographic evidence meant I didn't see it. I may as well have called him to say I had seen Bigfoot!

As I climbed higher into the mountains the views became more spectacular. Surrounded by high peaks and pine forests it was a special place to be. The road, however, wasn't particularly safe. Some of the vehicles coming down the mountain seemed to have forgotten how to use their brakes and took some of the sharp corners a little too close for comfort, but nothing was going to stop me from enjoying the moment. As I headed up the final mile of the last climb it suddenly occurred to me – I have run across the Rocky Mountains! I began to bubble with emotion and recorded it on the video:

"Well this is it! I've just come to the top of Cameron Pass, nearly two miles high. I've just run, climbed, walked, and crawled all the way across the Rocky Mountains! From here on in it's downhill all the way to New York City, from two miles high to sea level.

I'm a little bit happy today, I'm a little less happy with the 12-mile climb this morning, but hey we are at the top! Next stop New York City! USA! USA!"

I could see Sean in the distance. The significance of this point in the trip was clear in his face as I approached. He was beaming with pride! We both knew what I had endured to get to this point. This took so much out of me physically and emotionally that when we hugged at the top we both knew it was a turning point of our journey. We had been through deserts; we had climbed over the mountains; we could do anything! We treated ourselves with a cup of coffee and a ham sandwich, whilst speaking to a couple from Indiana, it was a wonderful moment to share with others. There were some times on the trip when I thought things couldn't get any better, so I was always surprised when they did.

What came as no surprise was the long downhill section after my arduous climb. I couldn't wait to open my stride and get some decent speed going. After my stop at the top I agreed with Sean that we would do six-mile checkpoints due to the downhill. As I set off down the mountain I had a big smile on my face. I hadn't had any significant downhill for a while. I was going to enjoy this.

After only 200 yards I was stopped in my tracks. Surprise time! In the distance I could see an animal eating grass on the riverbank. As it lifted its head I could see it was a moose. Here I was on top of a mountain in Colorado watching a moose eat by a crystal clear mountain river. I almost let out a little wee I was so excited. I climbed as quietly as I could down towards the river, surely the moose would take off as soon as it saw me. It didn't. I managed to get to a nice spot where I could sit and watch this magnificent creature. Every now and then he would lift his head and look at me. Probably thinking, what the hell is that dude staring at? I took the opportunity to eat some food whilst I was watching. I was having lunch with a moose. I even began to chat to him. (I think I'd gone a little mad at this point in the journey.) Such a peaceful few moments, BUT I still had at least 18 miles to run that day and I needed to move on. I said my goodbyes to my new friend, took a couple of pictures and slowly moved back to the highway. My day had been truly blessed. All I had to do now was make my way down the mountain.

From Cameron Pass the road took me into Poudre Canyon, which was about 60 miles long. Being in a canyon is quite a strange feeling. I had become used to looking far into the distance and being able to see for miles ahead, in a canyon it's like someone is watching over your shoulder, or looming above you. The road followed the route of the Poudre River and as I made my way down the mountain the river grew in size. Up by the moose it had been a gentle flowing stream but as I headed down the mountain the river became a powerful torrent. The noise was fantastic. Being near water is always a special thing. I think most people feel a sense of calm when they are near water. It became very soothing to the soul. Almost as though I had become part of it, I was following its path; the river was guiding me home.

The end of my first day in the canyon was spent at a campsite called Sleeping Elephant. When Sean told me I thought it was a ridiculous name for a campsite. He smiled at me and said you will see why when you get there. I was intrigued. I was certainly looking forward to getting to the tent as I had also just encountered my first canyon storm. Despite getting soaking wet it was pretty awesome. I could see the cloud formation coming over the canyon sides and gradually filling it up – a bit like a bath and I could see the rain coming up towards me. There was nowhere to hide I just had to accept I was going to get wet! I didn't mind I had had such a great day nothing could spoil it... apart from lightning! Thankfully, Sean drove back up the canyon for me to shelter. We were not prepared to take any chances with lightning. I waited until the storm passed before finishing the day.

"Oh, that's why it's called Sleeping Elephant." Opposite the campsite was Sleeping Elephant mountain, named because it looks like, you guessed it, a sleeping elephant! It actually does look like an elephant – it's pretty cool.

 FB post 30 June 2013 Theresa Daley
Loved meeting you and love what you are doing. God Speed!

We tucked into Sean's camping speciality of canned ravioli and cheese followed by a bit of music and chat. It was the end of our most perfect day yet!

Poudre Canyon proved to be a lot of fun. It was a busy week for us to be there. The fourth of July holiday was a few days away and lots of families made their way into the canyon to make use of the camping and rafting on the river. It was great seeing families out enjoying themselves and hearing kids laughing. I know that may sound strange but I had not heard a child laugh for a long time. It's a sound I am well used to at home with two young children. I love hearing my kids laugh and I really missed it.

The holiday traffic meant I had to be alert all day. Thankfully for me the traffic struggled to get any speed up as they travelled up the canyon especially towing some of the trailers they had, the size of some of the mobile homes was huge! Also there were no trucks on this road. I had now lost all commercial traffic to the Highway 40. I was pretty pleased about that.

Despite all the activity and beauty around me there was something that really started to get to me on my third day in the canyon. I couldn't see the horizon and I began to feel a little claustrophobic. I needed to get out. After a brief conversation with a local woman she told me I still had 20 miles of canyon left. I think I started to lose my mind a little as I began looking for possible ways to climb out. I'm sure I could manage to get a vantage point on top of one of the hills just to catch a glimpse of the horizon couldn't I? After about 20 minutes of sheer panic I managed to calm myself down. I would be out of the canyon in a few hours anyway so it wasn't worth risking a climb. I needed to try and relax and enjoy the last few miles and try to forget the word canyon! I did and was soon at the bottom. As I made my way along the road I dared to look back. Behind me in the distance the impressive solidity of the Rocky Mountains, in front of me were miles and miles of almost flat land. Although I was soon to find out it wasn't as flat as it looked it was certainly going to be flatter than the Rockies!

Fort Collins was to be our first big town after the canyon run. It was also the fourth of July, American Independence Day. We see the fourth of July celebrations on TV in the UK and it always looks immense. Lots of fireworks and partying going on, so Sean and I were both really looking forward to some real homespun American celebrations, yet before we could start the party we had to navigate through a pretty lively section of concrete highway. The ear plugs came out again as the noise of the traffic on the concrete was so loud. The volume of traffic also increased as the Highway 14 joined another. Add in to the mix a severe thunder and lightning storm and it was a pretty eventful few miles. I had to take cover for a few hours as this storm was pretty tasty and, funnily enough, I hadn't realised how scared Sean was of storms until I sat in the car with him. He was pretty freaked out at the close proximity of the lightning. We were pretty much like sitting ducks parked at the side of the highway so we decided to move on and get something to eat until the storm passed.

The great thing about storms in the States is that everything dries up very quickly. I was back out running within two hours being baked yet again in the early evening sun.

Fort Collins was not as I had expected. It was a fairly small place, although bigger than we had encountered for a while, sadly for us, all hopes of being involved in the huge July fourth celebrations were short-lived as there were none! As I ran through the town I saw very few people and no celebrations. I was pretty disappointed. I always like a party that celebrates beating the English! (sorry to my English friends) so I just cracked on and ran late into the evening. We had agreed to run until dusk, which happened to coincide with another McDonald's. Sean had been waiting in the car park for me to arrive and whilst he waited he watched the people coming through the drive through. One of the cars had a large dog hanging its head out the window. It is always funny to see a dog hanging out of a car window. It is even funnier when the dog falls out of the window as the car driver navigates the tight turn through the drive through. Yes folks, in his eagerness to stuff his face with burgers the owner of the dog managed to catapult his mutt clean out of the car. When I arrive ten minutes later Sean was still in fits of laughter. I wish he had managed to get it on video.

Although it had been a patchy day's running I was still pretty happy with my effort. The lack of fireworks was disappointing and, as a matter of fact, still annoys me now. The hotel didn't make up for anything either as it was yet another grotty place where sleep would be impossible due to other residents being annoying and loud.

Putting lack of holiday celebrations behind me I quickly made my way out of Fort Collins the next morning. I had been spoilt for some time with the lower mountain temperatures. Even though it had been hot there was usually a breeze that took the edge off. Coming out of the mountains and onto the flat again we were to get a taste of what was to come across the Midwest. It was hot! Literally burning your feet on the sidewalk hot (if there had been a sidewalk) but to my relief the horizon was back as I was out in open countryside with an uninterrupted view of the road east. Since leaving San Francisco I could always see mountains and now there was nothing between me and the curved horizon line, just miles and miles and miles to run. The road was a quiet one and, once again I got to grips with solitude. After the busy canyon road it was a nice change.

Making my way through a town called Windsor felt quite bizarre. Back in the UK Windsor is home to a royal castle and has often appeared to me to be a town full of upper class snobs, thankfully this was not the case here, it seemed a very nice place to live with a beautiful high street, charming shops and cafés. I got talking to a couple of people who seemed nice and supportive but my favourite conversation was with a couple of teenagers. In the UK if you try and speak with most boys between the age of 13 and 16 you will usually be greeted with a grunt. As I approached two young lads who looked about 13 or 14 years of age I said hello. "Well good morning sir, I hope you are having a nice day." I was slightly taken aback by the politeness of this young man. I am sad to say I reverted back to being a teenager and just grunted back at him. He now probably thinks all adults are idiots!

We were in a good routine by the time we hit the outskirts of the college town of Greeley. I arrived in the early evening and the town was pretty quiet, which was probably to be expected as the university was shut for summer vacation. As I went further through the town I got an uneasy feeling about the place. This was no Steamboat Springs. Some of the neighbourhoods I ran through made me pick up my pace a little. I don't know what it was but there seemed to be an atmosphere in the air. The locals didn't smile or look up most of the time. As nightfall came I finally lost my bottle and called Sean to pick me up. I didn't want to run at night in this town. It did have a great burger joint though and the hotel had a nice indoor pool so it wasn't a total disaster.

There was nothing but countryside for the next section of highway. I had been spoilt with the fresh mountain air and the lower temperatures (when I say lower I mean below 30 degrees); it had still been warm but it had been a little more bearable, but from Greeley to Fort Morgan the mercury started to rise. Mid-thirties and even as high as 40 was now the average daytime temperature. People had told me that if I thought Nevada was hot then I would be cooked alive by the time I hit Kansas. I thought these people were absolutely crazy. Nevada was the hottest place on earth, so I knew in my head I would be able to cope with Kansas. As I neared the Mid West I was starting to realise that these people were not crazy, it was actually going to get hotter and more and more humid.

I allowed myself some time to reflect here at the halfway point. Fifty days on the road with fifty to go. Reflection is a double-edged sword though, which, if you are not careful, can take you down. On one hand I was happy that we had made it to the halfway point relatively unscathed but I was also very hard on myself about my lack of daily mileage. It's very difficult to understand how hard I was on myself at times. At the end of the day it was me doing the running so there was no one else to blame. Although, I did try and blame everything and everyone else before I realised that it was all down to me.

I took the time to reassess the entire situation. I needed to be more realistic of how we were going to manage to hit the daily target. I was never going to be able to run through the hottest time of the day. I needed to establish a routine that allowed me to rest in the afternoon. This meant getting out of bed a little earlier but it was not as easy as it sounded. Sean did not enjoying getting up at seven o'clock let alone six. I was also struggling to get to sleep due to the amount of pain I was in each night. The thought of starting running at seven a.m. did not fill me full of joy either. I knew though that if I was ever going to make it to New York on time now was the moment to stop being such a baby and man up a little. The plan would be to start as early as possible, rest in the afternoon, then back out and finish the day. This routine would constantly change as the run went on but this was the starting point of my awakening to the fact that if I didn't adapt I would fail. Charles Darwin wrote once, "It is not the strongest of the species that survives, nor the most intelligent but rather the one most adaptable to change." I needed to adapt or risk failure. I don't do failure.

All went well for the first few mornings. Sean was on the ball with getting up and sourcing breakfast. I was up for the early start, as it meant I would be able to get a little coolness on my skin before the baking heat of the day melted my mind and not just my mind, the heat was literally melting my shoes. The comfort of the first few weeks in Utah, where I had bought new trainers, had long gone. The Rockies and the heat had more or less destroyed all my running shoes, so it was time for a new pair and there wasn't much between me and St Joseph Missouri; a town called Fort Morgan was my only hope.

After a tough morning on the road I agreed to meet Sean and have a look in the town for a sports store. I had set my mind on a pair of Nike Air Pegasus. These had been a great addition to my kit in Utah. They had given me great support and comfort over lots of miles. How hard could it be to find a pair of Nikes in America? Un-bloody-believably this town had every pair of running shoes but the ones I wanted. After several tortuous exchanges with shop assistants trying to tell me what I wanted and offering me advice on running I managed to find a store that had just been sent a new shoe by Adidas. The Adidas Energy Boost. This shoe, without doubt, changed the run completely. As soon as I tried them on I instantly said they are 'the ones'. Seriously, I can't tell you how good the next few miles felt. Again, I could run almost pain free. At the end of the day's mileage my feet didn't feel like they had been smashed with a hammer. Oh boy was I thankful for Adidas Boost. The rest of Colorado was going to be a breeze. Although our ability to get out of bed on a morning would only last a few days – Sean quickly lost his newly found energy and I kind of followed.

CHAPTER 11
Nebraska

1,621.65 miles to go
'Cookiegate'

Our route through Nebraska was a short one and only lasted for around 20 miles or so. The decision to take Highway 14 through Walden had left me higher on the map than planned, so it was a fairly straightforward route along Highway 34 until we got to the town of Haigler, where we would turn off onto Highway 27 until we reached St Francis in Kansas. There we would pick up the originally planned route on Highway 36.

Bubbling under for a few days, the tension between me and Sean was rising again. I was growing increasingly stressed at our lack of finance. Having successfully got this far I was becoming very worried that the only thing that might end our journey would be running out of money. I was holding on to my frustration that we had struggled to gain any further finance since the trip had begun and, added to this, one of my sponsors was having difficulties paying. We had to keep a check on every dime and ensure what we had went further than ever and, along with my financial concerns was my irritation with Sean's inability to get his arse out of bed on a morning. I needed him to be on the ball first thing in, sorting out bags and getting breakfast. Instead I was waiting for him to get up. I'm sure some days he would have just laid there all day had I let him. I know he was tired and struggling from being on the road for so long but hey, so was I! At least he didn't have to run thirty plus miles a day. There was also the issue of Sean's over-ordering and leaving food untouched at meal times. This annoys me even at home. Leaving food is a sin in my eyes! I had tried to explain to him that if he wasn't hungry he didn't need to order the food. Couldn't he wait until he was hungry rather than wasting it? He had done this again in Wray, the last stop in Colorado.

We had a Mexican meal, half of which he didn't eat. It really made me quite angry. On reaching the border of Nebraska the next day we decided to organise some lunch in Haigler. I always liked having a good break at lunch and if there was a good enough restaurant then we would always have a good feed. Thankfully, there was a super little café, as a matter of fact I think that's all there was in Haigler! Apart from one of the smallest jail cells I have ever seen – thankfully, no longer in use.

We did our usual of ordering a big burger and fries to sustain us for the rest of the day. Sean quite clearly wasn't hungry. He started shuffling around on his plate like you do when you are eight! "Are you going to eat that burger, Sean?" I could feel my blood rising! "I'm not really that hungry," was his reply. What happened next was what I call a controlled explosion. I let fly about how him not eating his food was a complete waste of our sponsors' money and I was fucking tired of it! I did this whilst in full control and I tried not to bring to the attention of the other diners that I was about to commit murder over the dinner table. I got up and left the café in a bit of a temper, "I will see you at the state line!"

The state line was only a few miles up Highway 27 and I had hoped to have calmed down by the time I got there. When I did arrive Sean seemed completely oblivious to the issue. He stood there asking what my problem was. This is where controlled explosion goes nuclear.

"It's about you wasting food and money you fucking idiot! I'm fucking tired of watching you waste food! I will show you waste!" at this stage I must have looked like an escapee from an institution. I opened the boot of the car and started to throw things out of the cool box. I found a big bag of cookies, which were Sean's favourite. I grabbed the bag and threw them out all over the ground whilst jumping on them! If you have ever seen the sketch from the TV show Fawlty Towers where John Cleese starts to hit his car with a tree branch you'll get the picture. I threw the remaining biscuits into a field and then myself into the car, where I sat trying to calm myself down.

This turned out to be one of the key moments of the whole trip.

I had always felt sure that Sean was more than capable of finishing the trip but in the back of my mind I was worried that, given the right situation, he would hatch an escape plan – I was potentially one argument away from me being stranded in the middle of America without support. I had made no provision for this eventuality, so it was always a nerve-wracking time when a row started. That's not to say I ever held back. Those people that know me will tell you I rarely hold back if something or someone pisses me off! I would like to be able to sometimes as it is something that gets me into trouble quite often. This time I had definitely over-stepped the mark. I cannot justify my actions, now or then, but to be fair I was under a little bit of pressure and Sean bore the brunt of it again!

The miles down to Highway 36 were quiet. We didn't speak at the checkpoints or on the phone. I got on with my job not knowing whether I was going to be ditched as soon as I got to the next town. Feeling isolated and vulnerable on a trip like this is not a nice feeling. You start to think that schemes are being hatched and conversations are happening that you have no control over. By the time my day of running was finished I had managed to convince myself that Sean had bought his plane ticket and was leaving that night.

I had directly challenged Sean. Now, he could do his usual thing and quit at the first sign of trouble or he could stick two fingers in the air and say, "Fuck you Tom, I'm staying!" When I say his 'usual thing' I don't want you to think that Sean is a quitter but he will be the first to admit that he rarely finishes anything he starts and, quite apart from raising his son Jude, he rarely gives anything 100 per cent. We did some circuit training in Wakefield before flying to America as part of our 'bonding' process. Sean would find it difficult to get to a stage where he would actually break sweat – he had usually quit well before then. I would finish the session having thrown up and feeling like death, joining him as he walked out of the gym like nothing had happened.

We were saved by a lady called Kerrie. When I say WE were saved I really mean THE WHOLE TRIP.

We had finally made it on to Highway 36, which would take us all the way through to Illinois. The first town on this road was St Francis. Apart from the tension Kansas was bloody hot, although it would get hotter, and I decided we both needed a break. We met at a gas station on the edge of town and Sean did his usual shopping duties – buying soda, chocolate and a map of Kansas. He seemed to be taking forever and after about 10 minutes he came out of the store with nothing in his hands. My heart sunk, my first reaction was that our credit cards had been declined. He got into the car and told me that the lady in the store had called the local newspaper about us and they would like to do a story about our journey. This is the first time Sean and I had spoken since lunchtime and it was awesome news. All across America we had had very little interest from the press – to be fair we didn't encounter many people let alone newspapers. We both laughed that we had gone from being ready to kill each other to discussing publicity in the space of 10 minutes. Sean took me back into the store to meet Kerrie, the lady who saved the trip.

CHAPTER 12

Kansas

1,581.65 miles to go
Saving grace

Kerrie was full of energy and welcomed me like a long lost friend. The store she ran was like a UK truck stop, made all the more busy because it was harvest time. Kerrie got us a drink and offered us a seat. This was my first real taste of Mid Western hospitality. She explained that as it was such a small town the reporter for the newspaper was busy and that she was going to write the story. Now that is what you call a true community newspaper – written for the people by the people. I found it all a little bit surreal being interviewed for a newspaper in a town where we had only just arrived. If only my own local newspaper back home had been as keen.

We chatted for an hour or so about everything from my drinking days to the recent row in Nebraska. Sean chipped in too and it was good to talk about how we both felt to someone who genuinely cared about our cause and it transpired that Kerrie's life too had been touched by addiction. After our interview and a few photographs we left to find our motel. Both Sean and I had been brought back together by Kerrie, our 'saving grace' and I knew that Kansas was going to be a great state for us. I also knew that Sean was in it for the long haul. He had finally quit on quitting.

We decided to take the evening off as we felt the pressure of the day had taken its toll. To be honest I was cooked. The temperature had hit 40 degrees that day and it was showing no signs of getting any cooler. The warnings about the heat of Kansas had been totally correct, I was so wrong to not believe them! It was like standing in front of an oven. No, I will change that statement; it was like being stood inside an oven with the door shut! I nicknamed Kansas the devil's kitchen – it was beyond any normal person's ability to run in those conditions. It's a good job I am not a normal person.

I had finally passed the halfway point of the trip; however, reaching the 50-day mark was a bit of a shock, as I realised that I was a long way behind schedule. I hate being late. Everywhere I go I am usually way too early. Orla and Oliver have given up arguing about setting off for school before time – it's just who I am. So, back to my favourite Darwin quote, I needed to adapt again and fast. If I carried on the way I was going I would not get to New York on time, even though in my head I was content to keep battling away, the intense heat was the game changer. I was going to suffer badly over the next few weeks unless I could find the motivation to change what I was doing.

In front of us a landscape of wheat fields fanned out as far as the eye could see and everywhere was alive with harvest activity. And boy did they know how to harvest! In some of the fields we saw four combine harvesters toiling with giant tractor and trailer units that looked like they had been built by NASA. Some of these fields appeared to be the size of my home city of Wakefield and the whole scale of the operation was of military proportions.

Running through Bird City, which is not a city at all, I managed to find an ice cream parlour. I devoured a large tub of mint choc chip. The owners of the shop didn't say anything but did look puzzled at a runner being out in the heat of the day. It was the first time for a while I began to question my own sanity. Having cooled off with the ice cream and resigned myself to the fact I was actually insane I moved on. I was heading for the town of Atwood where we would hopefully find a place to sleep and some food. The place was like a ghost town – there was just no one around. Having searched for a takeaway we found a Pizza Hut. I was pretty hungry so we decided to push the boat out and have a sit down meal. We were the only people in the place. The lady serving us again was super friendly. A lot like Kerrie from St Francis, she showed great interest in my run. After taking our order she came over to us and asked if we minded her calling the local newspaper to do an interview. I was so happy with this type of response. The people of Kansas really got what I was trying to do. I was happy to do a story. Now towns like Atwood have not got a large population so the newspaper is not on the scale of the *Guardian* or the *Telegraph* in the UK, but for me it was a chance to get my message of recovery to as many places as I could. The journalist arrived and over the next hour we shared our story of adventure. The great thing was that this lady had a great knowledge of the local area. I could have listened to her for hours as she told us about the history of the town. I loved the fact that it was an almost crime-free town, with little unemployment. This sleepy little town was actually home to quite a considerable number of millionaires. When I asked where everyone was she replied, "It's 115 degrees out there, everyone is inside with the air con on. Only an idiot would be outside in this heat!" she gave me a wry smile, which I ruefully acknowledged. And she was, of course, right. I was an idiot for being out in those kind of temperatures. I needed to start running outside the hottest time of the day. I needed to break my own rules and start running at night.

That night we sat in the motel deciding on a plan. I would run through the day until around three or four in the afternoon and then go back out at around eight o'clock and run into the night. Even the night temperatures would be high but they felt manageable without the sun burning your skin. This was the only way I could keep the mileage high without keeling over in the heat.

Over the next few days I ran until early afternoon and then rested. This was made easier as the towns along the highway were helpfully spaced out at 30-mile intervals and it was the best stretch we'd had as far as motels went. This meant I could get out of the sun and get some quality sleep before heading back out on the road. Good in theory, in practice this was not a perfect strategy. Running at night increased the risk of being injured or even killed. Whilst I enjoyed running at night at home under the amber glow of streetlights, I was not that keen on running down Highway 36 in pitch black. The drivers struggled to see me during the day, so at night they would have no chance. I don't blame the drivers. We drive to our surroundings and in America there are very few runners stupid enough to run at midnight. A driver would not be expecting to see a bearded idiot running directly towards them sporting a bright orange jacket and a head torch. They just would not be looking out for me. For this reason I doubled my attention span whilst running at night and treated every vehicle as a potential weapon. Mind you, it wasn't all bad, I very quickly realised that when the sun went down in Kansas the animals came out to play.

The noise at night from the crickets right across the States was always loud but in Kansas it was deafening. Even though I was on my own I never felt lonely. The noise was actually quite comforting. Add to this the reflections from the eyes that look back towards you from the fields and you've got a pretty special combination. It was a little scary for the first few nights, as I had no idea of what was actually looking back at me. As usual my mind did overtime for the first few hours every night thinking that I was being watched by a bear or a tiger (that's how my mind works sometimes!).

Probably the scariest moment was during my first night run. As I ran along the highway I could see something about 20 feet away. My head torch caught a flash of colour. I instantly stopped. I hope that's not a snake – the thought went through my head. Only it was a snake coiled up in the middle of the road. Apparently they do this at night as the tarmac is still warm from the heat of the day. Snakes are scary enough in the daytime but at night they take on a different level of horror! I stood frozen to the spot. I didn't want to go anywhere near it. We had ourselves a Mexican standoff… Come on Thomas, its time to face your fears! I started to move forward slowly and, as I got closer, I knew something wasn't right, could it be dead? I shone my torch directly over it to discover that, though it was still coiled, it had been squashed flat straight across the middle by a truck. With a quick jump for joy I ran off as quickly as I could. I didn't want its spirit following me and biting me on the bum! Honestly, the snake incident did scare me. I found it hard to settle for the rest of the night and over the next few weeks it wouldn't take much to make me anxious while running at night.

Having the towns so evenly spaced was an absolute Godsend. Throughout the previous states sourcing accommodation and food became a bit of a chore. Throughout Kansas I was sure that we would always be able to get a cheap motel and some food. It was never about finding good motels or quality food, our budget didn't allow for that, as long as we could find a bed and a gas station pizza we were happy. I think too, knowing that we had a new town every thirty miles or so kept our spirits up. What would it be like? How big would it be? Would it have a McDonald's? Yes folks, McDonald's became a longed-for establishment; it was not the food we were attracted to, no, it was the free Wi-Fi! How the modern traveller has changed their priorities. As our mobile phone signal was usually pretty poor, getting a fast internet connection was fantastic. Updating Facebook and Twitter was our only link to the outside world, subsequently Sean had become a bit of a Facebook addict since leaving San Francisco. Whilst there he scoffed at the ridiculous amount of time both Connor and I spent updating our status and here he was two months later pulling his hair out if he couldn't load up a post!

Arriving in Norton I saw the 'majestic' golden arches of McDonald's. Sean had already seen it and was in the car park getting his social media fix. It was a welcomed sight as the mercury was pretty high again.

Alongside the Wi-Fi and the food the air conditioning was awesome! Sean did the usual and went to get my order whilst I connected to the Social 'IV' line. I also got chatting to another traveller called Hope who was cycling across the country. Being able to share experiences was a great thing. Hope was travelling from east to west so she could tell me what was ahead and I could also do the same for her; she was also one of those people whose enthusiasm for life is infectious. You could tell she loved life even though at times life had not been kind to her. The reason for her journey was to raise funds for her best friend who had sustained a brain injury in a recent car accident. Hope invested so much time into making sure her friend was happy. She showed a real love and was determined that her friend would get everything she needed for the future. We ended up talking for over an hour. Sean became a little bit smitten with Hope. I think she opened his eyes to how you can make a positive out of every negative. I was glad we met her as it gave Sean something to focus on other than annoying me! Next town on our route was Smith Centre and Hope mentioned the lovely time she had had there with the locals. My experience of Smith Centre, however, was a little different.

After a decent day's running I had rested well and was ready to attack the night. We had decided to maximise the effort of going out at night by adding any mileage done after midnight to the next day's total. It was purely psychological of course and would not get me to New York any quicker, it just meant I was making the most out of my effort. I figured if I stayed out until three a.m. I could get between six and nine miles done depending on how I was feeling. This, in my head, would make the next day's job a little easier. This particular night was hot. Even at midnight it was 36 degrees. Despite the heat I always had my long sleeve orange running jacket on, together with my head torch, and when car headlights hit me I lit up like a lighthouse on the highway. The majority of cars passed on the other side of the road giving me a polite pip of the horn as they went past. Some even stopped to ensure I was OK and if I needed any help. I found this a little un-nerving the first time as you never know who is pulling up. Some crazed dude in a pick-up etc. They were nothing like that, just really nice people genuinely concerned for my safety. They always left smiling and laughing when I told them my story. "Hey man, you're crazy but good luck to you!" was usually the response.

This mood changed at about one-thirty a.m. just outside Smith Centre. I was running well when I saw the lights from a small pick-up truck. I was alert and saw that the driver didn't appear to have seen me. I could usually tell, as they would cross the rumble strip onto the other side of the carriageway. I flashed my head torch up and down and side to side in order to attract the driver's attention. This usually worked quite well. Not on this occasion. The driver continued at quite a speed almost driving on the shoulder of the highway and coming directly for me. I jumped into the ditch to avoid being hit, as I did so the driver must have finally spotted me and hit the brakes. The noise was deafening as they skidded out of control down the road, finally coming to a stop about 20 metres from where I had jumped into the ditch. "Get off the road ya stoopid bastard!" came a shout from the truck.

"You're gonna get yourself killed!"

"First of all the word is stupid and second, maybe if you opened your eyes you would have seen me running towards you, you fucking idiot!" was (what I felt) my rather controlled response.

"What the fuck are you doing running at night on the highway? Get on the country roads!"

"I am allowed to run on the highway at any time I want, ya prick, and the country roads go in the wrong direction, so mind your own business, open your eyes and fuck off!"

I heard the truck door opening, this guy is going to try to fight me, I thought. The man then stood at the side of his truck shouting all sorts of abuse at me. I am not having this I thought and ran towards him having finally lost my cool. "If you want to fight then that's what you will have ya fucker!" I screamed. The colour drained out of this guy's face. A six foot bearded runner hurtling towards you in the middle of the night must have been quite scary. He quickly jumped in his truck and screeched off calling me a crazy mother fucker! He was wrong. I am not crazy, I just don't tolerate bullies.

I was left standing alone angry and a little shaken up. I had nearly been killed by a careless driver and then almost got into a fist fight at the side of the road. I hadn't signed up for this. I knew what I was doing had a certain amount of risk but this brought it home to me how vulnerable I actually was. It suddenly occurred to me that if I had have been hit by that pick-up he probably wouldn't have stopped and I would have been lying there injured for some time. It also occurred to me that during the altercation the man could have easily produced a gun or a crowbar and again I would have been defenceless. I didn't want to put myself in this situation. I was annoyed with myself for getting involved in an argument at the side of the road. I had some serious thinking to do. By the time I reached Sean he could see I was pretty shaken up by the whole situation. We decided to finish for the night and would discuss things in the morning when I had calmed down.

I didn't sleep well at all that night, only managing to drop off around four a.m. At breakfast we discussed what had happen and both agreed that even though the incident was serious we shouldn't let it affect our progress as I had managed to get some good mileage in over the previous few days. We agreed a deadline of one a.m. to finish running and also agreed to have more frequent checkpoints. We had been doing a stop every four miles and after dark we would reduce that to two. This gave Sean a better idea of timings and if anything did happen I wouldn't be waiting long before he would come looking for me. Thankfully, we also managed to get better phone reception so we also agreed I would text if I was behind schedule. Putting these measures in place set both our minds at ease. We both also stood firm that we would not be driven off the road by some redneck idiot who couldn't drive.

Needing a little distraction we took some time off the next day to go to the geographical centre of the 48 states. Quite a strange place with a flagpole and the smallest church I have ever seen. It was still pretty cool to know we were at the centre of this great nation and it allowed me to gather my thoughts and forget about the previous evening. Wherever we went God was with us. I needed to start remembering this.

Things started to settle quite quickly after our short stop. I got back into my rhythm. The heat was still killing me but I was managing to do some decent mileage through the daytime, heading back out on the road around sixish and the difference was remarkable. I was managing to fit 16 miles in about five hours, which was around an hour faster than the daytime mileage. The nights were being kind to me now the only down side was the lack of sleep. I always struggled sleeping after a night run. My body was in so much pain I had to wait for the painkillers to kick in and for my adrenaline to dissipate. Some nights I would be still awake at three a.m. I even resorted to a painkiller sleeping tablet combination but only for two nights as I really struggled to wake up the next day. The best solution was earplugs. They just allowed me to cut out any noise like the air con or Sean and his night terrors (not sure we'll go into those...).

The further east we moved the more independent cafés appeared for breakfast. In Mankato we had a wonderful moment when we stopped to ask a lady for directions. This little old dear was watering the plants outside the bank when Sean approached her. "Excuse me can you tell me where we can get some breakfast around here?" I was not expecting what happened next. In a voice I can only describe as Foghorn Leghorn (the cartoon rooster) she replied, "Oh yeah, up the road at the Red Rooster," she said it so loud and in such a voice I pissed myself laughing in the car. I think Sean heard me and also got the giggles.

"How will I know where it is?"

"There's a big red rooster outside!" By this stage I was falling out the car laughing. As soon as Sean got back in the car there was uproar. The poor lady must have thought we had gone mad! We arrived at the Red Rooster, an old style transport café, to find an ambulance in the car park – never a good sign at an eating establishment. We were hungry though so went in anyway to be met by a scene from the movie *Cocoon*. I mean this in the nicest possible way but Sean was the youngest person in the place by about 50 years, apart from the paramedic and the doctor tending to an elderly gentleman who appeared to have just had a stroke. It was quite a strange atmosphere as you can imagine. The lady who ran the café came over with coffee and said she would get our orders when the man had been stretchered out. Seriously, I am not making this up. It was almost an out of body experience – surely this is not actually happening to me? I only want breakfast. The gentleman was eventually taken to hospital where I hope he made a full recovery. I am sure he did.

"What can I get you?" the kind lady asked. Now, I find it hard to gauge sometimes how far to take humour and on this occasion I think over-stepped the mark "Certainly not the same as that gentleman had!" There was a momentary pause when I thought I was going to be kicked out when suddenly the lady started to chuckle. Phew, she had a sense of humour. She turned out to be a cracking host who made us laugh, especially when she said we looked like a couple of 'Polaks'! She was happy to have some banter and fed us well. She even put on Elton John's 'Candle in the Wind', when she found out we lived in England – I didn't have the heart to tell her my views on the monarchy. The hour we spent in the Red Rooster was such a boost.

By this stage Kansas was becoming a bit of a toil. I knew it was the last really big state and if I could get this one out of the way it would become mentally easier to manage the smaller states. My concentration levels had dropped considerably and I was becoming bored. The monotony of the same vast fields and big skies for miles and miles left me needing a fresh view, but this sort of thinking got me nowhere in a hurry. I had to constantly remind myself that I needed to concentrate on each day, one day at a time. I took whatever entertainment I could. Not that Sean appreciated it sometimes...

A quite amazing natural entertainment were the storms in Kansas, they were awesome. I would normally say thunder and lightning storms but in Kansas it was usually one or the other, rarely would we get them together. The electrical storms were killers. Across the open plains you could see for a couple of hundred miles as the ferocious forks of lightning lit up the sky. They were usually a long way from us so I had no worries running. On one occasion, however, a storm did get rather close. I could see it approaching from behind me. "I will outrun it," I said to Sean, "I just have to keep the pace up."

Sean looked at me as though I was crazy. "Tom we agreed that we wouldn't run in an electrical storm."

"I am not, it's 20 miles behind me, it'll be OK!" In my head this was a perfectly harmless thing to do, to out run an electrical storm. What an idiot!

Every now and then the night sky lit up, it was amazing. There was no rain or thunder just an amazing crackling power in the air. It seemed to energise me. I began to run quite smoothly and was enjoying a bit of healthy competition. I would not allow this storm to catch me. Sean had the full view, the panorama of the Kansas skyline lit up by electrical flashes, whilst knowing his brother was dodging the strikes! He would call on the mobile, "That was a bit close!" I would tell him it was fine. Every checkpoint he would try and convince me that we had done enough for the evening. Every checkpoint I would smile and move on. I was loving it. At one stage I had a bit of fun with him by saying "God is with me, nothing can stop me!" I think he saw this as me testing the power of God and that really didn't sit well with him. After a few hours of being chased through the plains of Kansas I decided I had done enough. I had won that race, the storm had gone and I was still alive. Oh boy was I alive. It was the most fun I could have with my clothes on!

I didn't dare push my luck after that. The morning after I realised how stupid I had been. Running in an electrical storm is not smart. I knew I had got lucky. From then on as soon as an electrical storm appeared I called Sean and we waited it out in the car. For a few days the black storm clouds would gather and I would spend at least an hour a day hiding from the rain or the lightning. Again, like everything in the States, Kansas rain was crazy stuff. It would deluge more rain in an hour than we had seen all year in the UK. The good thing was you could see it coming and had time to prepare.

Highway 36 was slow progress. I fully appreciated the size of America by this stage. Even though I was getting through some good mileage I never appeared to get any closer to the state line. To keep my sanity I made sure that I laughed as often as possible, even at the most ridiculous things. Coming across a place called Home made me laugh a lot. I began singing about the yellow brick road and managed to convince myself that I would see the tin man, a lion and a scarecrow before the day was out. Funnily enough it did get me thinking about home. I had tried not think too much about my family whilst I was running as it upset me. Running through Home I could think of nothing else. Home is a very special place and it is something I have struggled to find for many years. Leaving Ireland at 11 left me confused as to where my home was. When we returned on holiday I would always say I was going home but once I got there people would refer to us as being Yorkshire kids. In Yorkshire I was the Irish kid. I struggled to belong. I think I have only recently found it with Zoë. I only really started to feel part of a home when I stopped drinking. Since then every year my foundations of home have become stronger and I now feel that I am in a good place with a strong home life. Zoë and the children are central to that, it is not the bricks and mortar that make a home, it is the people in it. I missed those people so much that day.

Minor meltdowns were not too uncommon throughout the trip but Kansas saw one or two. I think the combination of the heat, the night running and the sheer scale of what I still had left to do took its toll. As I approached Hiawatha, close to the state line, I came close to giving up. It had once again all become too much. This time though I didn't take it out on Sean, I just lay on the bed in the motel and moaned. Lo and behold it was Sean who finally stepped up to the plate and ripped the shit out of me. He told me to get a grip and just get on with the job. Do the 36 miles per day and we will see what happens. It seemed to work as I spoke about it in my video diary.

"Well it's the night of day 63 and I've had a bit of a kicking off, well not a kicking, a bit of motivation from Sean.

"Lying in the hotel room, didn't want to go out, didn't want to do any running, really feeling down. Can't do this, too many miles to do, too short of time. Pissed off looking at maps and mileage.

"I've just got to keep doing what I'm doing, that's what he said, 'just do your 36 a day and see where we are at.'

"So we are out again this evening going to do some miles and hopefully that will get us to 36 for the day and I can shake myself for tomorrow.

"Speak to you soon."

Looking back on this I was very proud of Sean's reaction that night. It would have been very easy for him to kick his feet up and say, "Whatever, your call," but he didn't. He chose to stand up and take control of the situation. He kicked my arse and got us moving again. For me it was a great moment, knowing that Sean had found his voice. I kicked on that night and managed 34 miles. This took us in to the town of Hiawatha, which, even though there was not much there, deserves a mention just for the cool name!

The final push towards the Missouri river and the state line was dotted with minor towns and not much else, just more fields, endless horizons. Even running through Troy didn't spark any life into me. Kansas had been tough physically and mentally, and, at the time I was glad to see the back of it, but thinking about it now I loved my time in that great state, the state where you are never alone!

CHAPTER 13

Missouri

1,213.15 miles to go
One bite at a time

 @MrMarkBeaumont
Check Tom Fitzsimons @dryingout as he runs across America –
'only' ran marathon today!! #run4sobriety #youradventure

When I decided to write this book and split the journey between states I was kind of dreading this one. I don't want to upset anyone from Missouri but, for me this state sucked big time! It may have been my mental state at the time but I didn't like this place at all.

After crossing the wide, flat waters of the Missouri River I negotiated the busy roads of St Joseph. St Joseph is a busy city with lots of angry drivers. I had been spoiled throughout Kansas. Apart from my less than friendly late night encounter outside Smith Centre, the roads and drivers of Kansas had been gentle on me. St Joseph was different. It had a feel of a big city with a tough underbelly. The areas I ran through just looked mean. The people I encountered on my first day in the city also looked mean. By the time I reached the hotel I'd had enough. It was time to lock myself away for 24 hours. I needed a rest. I found the city overwhelming. The noise from the traffic and the busyness of the shopping mall were all too much after the long lonely roads of Kansas.

The rest was a calculated risk. I was already behind schedule but I felt that if I didn't take a break I wouldn't be able to finish at all. I made the decision and put my feet up for a day of eating M&M's and drinking Dr Pepper. The key for me was staying out of the sun. After 70 days of sunshine

I was pretty glad when I could get away from it for a long period of time. I did dip in the pool every few hours though just to ease my aching feet and legs! Sean used the time to find a barber shop and generally chill out for the day. I needed nothing from him that day apart from lunch, which he brought to the room. I really enjoyed my rest days. 'NCIS' marathons became a favourite as well as re-runs of 'Fast N' Loud!' Being able to have time to read all the messages of support that had been coming in through Facebook and Twitter was also a great morale boost. Knowing that people back home were following my journey meant so much to me. There are times on the road when you feel totally alone and having these messages meant I knew someone was thinking of me. Kansas had also messed up my sleep pattern, so I was pleased to get the chance to catch up on some much needed shut eye. I think, had I been given the opportunity, I could have gone to sleep for the rest of the year at that point.

I was pretty happy with my day off and felt so much better the next morning. I was ready to smash some miles in.

Sean did his usual coffee run early the next morning. Every motel across America seems to provide free industrial strength coffee to their customers. Sean loved this idea. I don't know whether he liked it because it was free or because he liked the coffee, either way it got him moving in the morning so I wasn't complaining. On this occasion he returned empty handed. This was not like Sean! He had gone to the reception for his freebie only to be confronted by a full blown domestic between a young couple who were fighting over their baby. The man appeared to be high on meth amphetamine and was insisting on taking the baby. The young girl was screaming that he was high and that the hotel staff needed to get the police involved. All this was going on with Sean standing there not getting involved just trying to get the attention of the motel staff to put some fucking coffee on! He failed and gave up leaving the young couple to fight it out in the lobby. Thankfully, the police arrived, dealt with the situation quickly, sadly there was still no coffee by the time we had checked out. McDonald's it was then!

Despite my day off and feeling better I still looked like shit. My t-shirts had seen better days and my beard was well on its way to being biblical. To be honest I had given up on my image. I had so little human contact on the road I felt it didn't matter that much. The only people who saw me were driving in trucks and cars at 60 miles an hour. It's funny, when you start to plan these trips image is always at the forefront of your mind. The right t-shirts and shorts, even the socks have to match your running gear. I have always been a bit of a snob when it comes to my running image, sometimes the phrase 'all the gear and no idea' springs to mind. By this stage I not only looked scruffy, I looked scary. I hadn't realised how bad I looked until I got back on the road again after my day off.

The road out of St Joseph's was quite difficult. There were lots of junctions to negotiate and lots of traffic. It became quite stressful as the drivers seemed a lot more aggressive than I had previously encountered. It was probably a city thing and I was pleased to meet Sean after five fairly stressful miles along a busy dual carriageway. Due to the traffic being so busy Sean had driven up a slip road and parked outside a church (I didn't like it when he couldn't just pull up at the side of the road, it felt like extra mileage). At the top of the slip road I crossed toward the car park and, as I did so, two young lads, about nine years old, were walking along the sidewalk. As they approached me they handed me some money, nine cents, and continued on their way. When I started to talk to them about what I was doing they looked at me as if I was an alien. One of them shouted "Yeah, yeah just don't gamble it." I was a little puzzled at the comment but was still happy for the encounter.

"They thought I was a tramp, the little bastards!" I shouted to myself as I made my way down the highway. The penny had finally dropped. As I approached the young lads they must have thought, oh shit it's a hobo, quick give him some money so he goes away. It was the "don't gamble" comment that made me realise. I must have looked like a real crazy idiot standing in the street shouting "I'm going to New York kids; I'm going to New York!" It made me realise that maybe it was time to start making an effort to tidy myself up.

Missouri was the state of endless cornfields and on continuously undulating roads I found it hard to find my rhythm, the roads were bloody ridiculous to be honest, sometimes they were more like roller coasters. I also remember Missouri as the state where the realisation of the task ahead really hit home. I was four weeks from success or failure. That's how I saw it. If I didn't get to Coney Island by August 27th I would have failed. Regardless of how far I had got it would have all been for nothing. In one of my video diaries I say I don't want to be the man who almost ran across the USA. So looking back I suppose I am quite thankful to Missouri, as it allowed me time to think and re-focus my efforts.

Despite my boredom my mileage was good. The first stop on the road was a Super 8 motel in Cameron. I had managed to do 36 miles and was feeling a little sore. As I waited in the car park for Sean to check us in I noticed a couple with a trailer full of old furniture, or more accurately junk. I was interested in why anyone would have so much junk piled up in a trailer, so I sauntered over and introduced myself and asked what all the stuff was. The couple were called Larry and Cindy. Larry turned all this 'junk' into bespoke furniture and Cindy had come along to provide the muscle during the loading process. Instantly the conversation turned to the run. They were extremely supportive of the whole trip and especially the issues surrounding addiction. They had a strong faith too, which they shared with me and spoke about the strength the Lord had brought to their own lives. Their son had done two tours of Afghanistan and I could see how very proud they were of him. Larry told me a story of how his son had been preparing for promotion and that he was finding it hard to cope with all the rigours of the tests. His father reminded him of a saying he had used throughout his childhood: "How do you eat an elephant? One bite at a time." His son had laughed and applied this principle and gained his promotion. I feel that Larry had told me that story for a reason. I believe he detected a hint of desperation in my voice as to how far I had to go and the fear of not making it. It was great to leave Larry and Cindy with that saying firmly planted in my head. I would get to New York "one bite at a time". It was a lovely meeting and I often think back to it.

As for the rest of Missouri, well nothing else happened apart from a couple of signs pointing to covered bridges that we never found. We were also quite disappointed that nothing more was made of Walt Disney's connection to Marceline. Disney lived on a farm there and developed his love for drawing in the area. Considering dear old Walt is probably one of America's most famous sons he seems to have been overlooked somewhat. There was a big deal, however, made out of General Pershing's birth place. Who? John Pershing was America's army commander-in-chief when America joined World War I in 1917. Born in Laclede, a nuclear missile was also named after him.

A little bit like one of my old school reports, Missouri can be summed up in three words: could do better!

CHAPTER 14
Illinois

1,015.95 miles to go
One steak at a time

 FB post 23 August Mark Aleman
Mark Aleman from Holiday Inn Quincy Illinois here. We are excited to have you coming to our property and will take great care of you while you are in Quincy. When I get a better fix on your arrival date I will alert our local media to your story. Until then I wish you great success!!

The mighty Mississippi river was within touching distance and the boredom of Missouri had been balanced out by putting in some great mileage to reach the state line. I was filled with excitement, the response we had already received from the people of Illinois had been awesome and I was really looking forward to running across this state.

To make it a little easier to cross the river I had taken a different route up towards Quincy, where we had also been offered a free night's accommodation from the Quincy Holiday Inn. The thought of staying in a decent hotel blew my mind. Although Missouri hadn't been that bad for motels, to be able to sleep in a smart hotel was going to be very welcome. The hotel manager, Mark, had also arranged for a local TV crew to meet me beside the Mississippi. Up to this point I had had no interest from any TV media at all, so this meeting was a big deal.

As I approached the river there were two bridges, neither of which allowed for pedestrians. I already knew this would be the case but held out hope that I would be able to run on the bridge without the authorities knowing. Sadly, there was no chance of this happening. The bridges were two lanes with no hard shoulder. By now I had become fairly ballsy when it comes to running on the highway but when the signs clearly say no pedestrians and when there appears to be no apparent route then sometimes you have to admit defeat and say no. I called Sean and got him to take me over the river.

To finally see the Mississippi was fantastic. A pretty impressive, vast expanse of water, instantly you could see that this was a working river with big cargoes being transported up and down its length. Playing an important role in the country's fortunes, the river was also an important milestone for me; crossing its waters meant that I was more than two thirds of the way across America – I could almost smell New York.

Bankside I was met by a lovely TV journalist called Kendra White from WGEM News. She was so enthusiastic about my journey. We chatted and did the interview within touching distance of the big river. I did feel like a bit of a celebrity, as the traffic slowed to see who was being interviewed. My usual free-flowing chat was a little rusty, as I hadn't spoken to anyone apart from Sean for such a long time. Kendra took her time and let me talk for as long as I needed to. The interview again allowed me to remember the importance of what I was doing. This was something that I needed, getting caught up in the day-to-day stress of the journey meant that sometimes I forgot the bigger picture. I was running for those who couldn't and I was in a privileged situation. Although I was glad of the media attention I also needed to get a few more miles in for the day and needed to keep pushing. Interview over, I continued on the road towards the hotel.

FB post 2013 Cindy Spake
Welcome to Quincy, Il Tom!

It was a big thing being able to stay in a posh hotel for the night. Up to this point we had stayed in pretty basic accommodation, which to be fair rather suited us. By this time, however, I looked like a complete hobo but when I arrived the welcome I received was overwhelming. Mark, the hotel manager, came to meet us and made me feel like a conquering hero. He too was a marathon runner and understood some of what I was feeling. He arranged our room and agreed to meet us for dinner. There are times when you meet people and they don't really listen to what you say or appear disinterested. Mark was not one of these people. Sean and I both looked at each other in the lift and both said, "He gets it." He fully grasped the whole concept of Run4Sobriety.

Having someone join us for dinner was something both Sean and I found quite strange. We were used to sitting in McDonald's not talking and making the most of the free Wi-Fi. Mark didn't actually eat with us but he sat down and shared our space, he listened, he spoke, he gave advice, he acted like a friend. For the first time since Utah we felt welcome. The dinner too was awesome. I remember taking a picture of the vegetables, as they were the first fresh veggies I'd had since leaving the B&B in Utah. We also had fillet steak, which was like heaven after so many burgers! I will be honest we stuffed our faces with so much food, including pudding, that I didn't know if I'd ever be able to run again. I slept like a baby in a big comfortable bed and felt refreshed and ready for the day ahead. Breakfast was another 'love in' with people making me feel so welcome. We took photographs in the lobby, said our goodbyes and hit the road again. It really is amazing what a difference this made to my mindset. I felt alive again. What we were doing was actually pretty damn great!

From Quincy we moved out along a series of country roads towards a small town called Meredosia. One of the drawbacks of eating good food after a long period of eating rubbish is that your body can't handle it and rejects it; either that or I had eaten something that seriously disagreed with me. I felt like I was dying. I had been vomiting for most of the day. I hadn't told Sean, as I didn't want to worry him – we couldn't really afford another day off. As soon as I vomited I would drink as much fluid as I could to try and stave off dehydration. This worked some times, at others it made things worse and I would projectile Gatorade across the highway. Eventually, we decided to take a break and to drive into town and find a motel. Well, in the same way that Quincy was posh Meredosia was not! It was a tough hard-working town with little to offer a traveller. The motel was 30 bucks a night and when I went into the room I could see why. It was dirty, "I think I will sleep in the sleeping bag tonight Sean." My fragile stomach actually felt a little better on leaving the room.

I knew that despite being under the weather I had to try and eat and the only place available in Meredosia was a small bar. It felt a little weird going into a bar with a Run4Sobriety t-shirt on but it had to be done. We were back to eating grease again with a big hamburger and fries. It seemed to do the trick for the first few miles at least. I felt strong again for a few hours until just before the small village of Chambersburg where the vomiting returned. This time in front of Sean as I approached the checkpoint. "This is why God has asked you to do this and not me brother! If that was me I'd be flying home by now," Sean said in a voice of disbelief.

I replied by saying, "One more mile."

After a good sleep in a grotty motel and a great breakfast I felt good to go the next morning. I hadn't quite made it past Chambersburg and there was 30 miles or so to Jacksonville. Getting into my rhythm, I was lost in my own little world when a Harley Davidson rider pulled up alongside me. I no longer found this strange as it had happened quite a few times, what I did find odd was what the rider said to me.

"Hey are you Tom?" How the hell did this dude know my name?

"Yes, I am."

"Hi, I'm Marty and I will be looking after you for the day."

Marty had been contacted through Facebook by Carol who was Mark's, (our fabulous Holiday Inn host) sister, with the hope that people along my route would come out and support me – Marty answered that call.

I had never expected the hospitality we were offered in Illinois. I felt a little awkward as I stood at the side of the road talking to this crazy dude wearing a Christian motorcycle club jacket. I think both Sean and

I viewed everyone with suspicion due to the fact we had had very little human contact for months. Marty quickly allayed those fears with a very supportive 'I'm here to help' attitude. After sharing some time with him at the side of the road I left him to make arrangements with Sean for later in the day. I had some big miles ahead. The contact made me smile as I made my way through Meredosia, where we had stayed in the night before and past our dodgy motel, probably the worst we had stayed in. I got stopped again in Meredosia to do an interview with a local journalist and I started to think that the day was going to be ruined by people. Then I remembered why I was doing it. I needed these people to help promote the run and the cause. Again, the lovely journalist seemed to get it. She treated us to a very tasty but early lunch, heard our story, took some pictures and wished us luck for the rest of the journey.

The landscape of Illinois was pretty much like Kansas with lots of swaying corn but it also had some lush greenery to break up the view with woods and grassy fields. The further east we travelled, the more hospitable the landscape. The unforgiving, hostile lands of Nevada and Utah felt a long way behind me. Street names also made me laugh a little. Why the hell would you call a road Spunky Ridge Road other than to make people laugh?

As I ended the day just outside Jacksonville I met Steve and Tiffany. Again, they had heard about my journey through Facebook and had come out to support me. To be honest I was almost ready for finishing the day before I met them, but their enthusiasm and interest in my journey was amazing. I walked with each of them as the other drove up ahead. It was nice to have some company on the road. We chatted and laughed and the miles seemed to fly by. What could have been a 29-mile day ended with 33 miles on the clock. At the last checkpoint Marty arrived to take us to dinner at his place and we arranged to see Steve and Tiffany the next day.

Sean and I had no idea what to expect, it's not often you go to dinner with a complete stranger but I think I am a pretty good judge of character and knew that Marty was a good man. I drove with Marty and

Sean followed. We took a tour of Jacksonville and I could tell that Marty was proud of the town he lived in. I have to say it had a nice feel to it. His house was on a lovely street and his wonderful wife Sue welcomed us warmly. She even laughed at my sunburn. We sat out on their patio and instantly felt relaxed. Marty was good company. Sean looked relaxed and I was pleased to be able to have a home-cooked meal. I was even more pleased when I saw the size of the steaks that Marty was cooking on the BBQ, they were huge! They must have been two inches thick and the size of a dinner plate. This would fuel me for a month. I was still a little weak from my sickness two days earlier but I knew I could handle this bad boy steak. Once Marty was happy the steaks were cooked to perfection we sat down to eat. Marty led us in prayer and almost made me cry with his words of faith. The warmth I felt that evening was something that has remained with me through the months since returning home. Sue and Marty listened and laughed and gave advice. They understood.

During our evening together Sean had been talking to Marty and Sue about his passion for American politics (something, I have to say, I had long since switched off to). Springfield, Illinois, was the next town, the resting place of President Lincoln, it was also the site of the Lincoln museum. Knowing this Marty did something above and beyond the call of duty. He gave Sean his museum pass and agreed to act as my support whilst Sean had the day off. Sean could hardly contain himself he was so excited at the prospect of time away from the run. I was so happy that Marty agreed to do it, as Sean had been under so much pressure that he deserved a day off. For Sean it was a once in a lifetime opportunity. Marty had also arranged for us to stay with another Holiday Inn who looked after us again so well. I felt like a celebrity.

The next morning Marty took us for breakfast at his favourite café. I had to laugh – it doesn't seem to matter where in the world you are, us men always have a favourite café! After the steak the night before I was surprised how much food I was able to consume. I was also the talk of the town, as the previous day's interview was front page news. The ladies in the café were talking and pointing until finally one plucked up the courage to ask, "Are you the guy on the front page of the paper?" They got very excited when I said I was and they asked me to autograph the paper. Embarrassed, I agreed. My first autograph!

Setting off that morning I was joined by Steve out on the road who cycled alongside me for the first ten miles of the day. Having company on the road was awesome, although I was quite envious of his bike! As soon as Marty appeared Sean disappeared in a big cloud of dust – it really did look a bit like the cartoon 'Road Runner'! Sean was gone and I was being crewed by someone new for the first time since the run began. Marty was great, he did exactly what was needed although he did take longer for a toilet break than is normally allowed (only joking Marty!). The new environment was good for me. I think it was good for both of us to have a break from each other. Sean and I had done everything together since the start. A few hours break was exactly what was needed. Later that day Sean returned full of useless bits of information about American presidents, but more importantly he was refreshed. Marty said his goodbyes and left us to push on.

Making my way toward Springfield along old Highway 36 I was in a reflective mood. So much had happened since I crossed the Mississippi I felt quite overwhelmed. Was I in danger of getting a little too used to the attention? I had built up a barrier over the previous weeks and months to protect myself from too much emotion; I could not allow myself to get caught up in feelings of happiness or sadness, I just had to run. Oddly enough, acts of kindness left me feeling very vulnerable. Over the past few days my heart had been awakened and I embraced that more human side of me that I knew had been lost since California. Realistically though, to keep going, somehow I had to return to the robotic numbness that forms part of being an ultra-runner.

Thankfully all feelings of humanity were extinguished when I arrived at our next hotel. We had been given a complimentary room at the

Crowne Plaza Hotel in Springfield. This was by far the swankiest hotel we had stayed in and, as I walked into the magnificent foyer, I began to feel like a stray dog that was trying his luck getting into a butcher's shop. I was dressed in my running shorts that were covered in sweat from the 30 miles run that day. My running shoes no longer looked in pristine condition and my beard was beginning to take on the look of a scary serial killer. I no longer felt human. The people on reception treated me fantastically well, it was just me that felt everyone was staring at me. Everything about me was screaming to go and have a shave and put on some proper clothes but I knew I still had a long way to go. The motivation from the staring and the whispers got me back into the right mindset. I was on my own and I needed to remember that.

Those feelings of doing this on my own were further brought home to me after a row with Zoë. It appeared that after 72 days on the road I had become something in the background. Zoë had taken on a new job before I left, and added to the responsibility of being a lone parent, she had done what most of us would do. She adapted to her surroundings and I felt like she had put me and the challenge in second place; if we needed something doing she would do it after she had dealt with all her shit! No one appeared to be looking at our finances, accommodation or routes. It all appeared to be falling apart. I couldn't do this on my own. I remember coming out of Springfield believing that I had run my last day. I was angry with Zoë and Sean. How could they not understand the importance of this run? Looking back I fully understand that it was *my* run. It was down to me. Those thoughts played heavily on me for a few hours. In fact Zoë and Sean had done and continued to do a fantastic job, my fatigued mind was playing with my reality and bubbling frustrations.

I returned to robotic ultra-runner mode almost instantly, as I realised that there was little I could do about the situation and being angry at people was not the answer. I also needed to concentrate, Highway 36 became quite a hazardous road at night and I had to be on high alert for rogue drivers. The fact is that in America drivers are more likely to encounter a deer than a runner, and let's face it no one cares if they hit a deer, apart from a little damage to the truck everyone is fine. Sadly, that leaves the lone runner vulnerable to late night drivers who are busy on their phones or playing with their car stereos. Despite being lit up like a Christmas tree I again encountered several cars racing toward me at high speed, 'not seeing me'. On one five-mile stretch of road I had to jump into ditches several times. The later it got the more I began to lose my nerve. I had passed a couple of small bars and it would seem that their attitude to drink driving was a little more relaxed than one would hope for; some of the cars passing were not exactly travelling in a straight line. My intention was to make it to the centre of Decatur that evening but I fell short by a mile or two and took cover in the safety of a nice motel.

Running through Decatur was slow going with lots of traffic and crossings to negotiate. I had learned my lesson from being knocked down in Colorado and knew that I needed to pay close attention to all drivers, regardless of whether I thought they had seen me or not. I found it hard getting into a rhythm and added to the heat, which was constantly around 30 degrees, I was moving at a snail's pace. The only thing that was keeping me going was the knowledge that we had yet another free night's accommodation in an Amish village called Arthur.

We had yet to encounter any of the Amish community and didn't expect to see any until we hit Pennsylvania. My only knowledge of them was some brief research about their lives before I left the UK. I was fascinated by their determination to avoid all modern implements and tools, including having no electricity or motorised vehicles. How could any group of people avoid these things in the USA? I also gained a slightly twisted view of Amish life from a Discovery Channel programme called 'Amish Mafia', which followed a so-called mafia boss who controlled, of all things, the maple syrup trade in his community. It all seemed a bit of a joke.

Steve and Tiffany had made all the arrangements and all we had to do was turn up in Arthur. We remained cautious of being offered places to stay and I was sure that one day our luck would run out and we would end up in a crack house, hiding in our sleeping bags, fearing for our lives. Thankfully, once again, our luck was in. We arrived in the picturesque village of Arthur, Illinois, and it was perfect. We were met by Marsha and Jeff who embraced us warmly. Their bed and breakfast was a small house at the side of their own beautiful home. I couldn't believe we had a whole house to ourselves. The fridge was full of juice and food, the beds were huge (well mine was) and yet again the people of Illinois had come up trumps.

Now, the trouble with all this hospitality is that we had to look reasonably smart for dinner. I had spent so much time in running gear I had almost forgotten what it was like to be fully dressed. I decided that going for dinner with Marsha and Jeff required a pair of jeans but after ten minutes I decided to change back into a pair of shorts. I didn't like the feeling of having long trousers on. It felt too normal. The only smart shorts I had were about two sizes too big for me, as I had lost nearly two stones, in weight since setting off from San Francisco. Still, it was as smart as I was going to get. Marsha and Jeff drove us to the local Amish restaurant, which as you can imagine on a Saturday night in a small town was a busy place. As we pulled up in the car park we could see that this town was not the usual mix of SUVs and mustangs. This 'car park' was full of horses and carts. Yes folk,s Saturday night in Arthur, Illinois, is the place to be with a horse and cart. We felt slightly out of place pulling up in Jeff's fantastic SUV, although I must admit I preferred it to a horse. It was such a great sight to see that the community was very much an Amish community but happily integrated with mainstream America.

The restaurant was owned and operated by the Amish, so all the staff were wearing the traditional clothing, which again felt a little strange knowing that this was not a uniform but clothes they chose to wear. Suddenly I didn't feel so insecure about my big shorts.

Whatever the dress code, the food was fantastic. A large buffet of meat and potatoes and those little seen things called vegetables. I was happy to stuff the plate high and savour the full flavours of the quality food. We chatted to Marsha and Jeff like they were long-time friends. Jeff was the type of guy you would like to have as a father. I instantly trusted him and was engaged by his every word. He is one of the good guys. Marsha was just so much fun! She laughed and asked questions and offered support and was a genuinely lovely person. The enjoyment of their company also meant that any prospect of an early night disappeared when we got back to the house and began to talk about our journey and life in general. We talked long into the night fuelled by coffee and cake, and only at the thought of the 35 miles I had to put in the next day did I call it a night. I think we could have talked until the sun came up.

Jeff and Marsha, Marty, Sue, Steve and Tiffany not forgetting Mark and the Holiday Inn Quincy staff made Illinois a very special place to spend time in. Leaving Arthur to hit the road the next morning was quite tough. I could have quite happily stayed there for... well forever really. I felt peace in that small community and hope to return one day.

Jeff had told us that his office was further up the road and that if we needed to use his internet or toilet facilities we were more than welcome. He gave us good directions and even showed us the location on Google Maps. I was pretty sure of where it was and how long it would take to get there. What neither Sean nor I spotted was that it was on the left-hand side of the road. Sean had done his usual thing of nodding his head saying he was listening and understood etc. so, you can imagine my confusion when I see Sean pulled up in someone's yard a few miles up the road on the right-hand side. Jeff was just pulling out of the yard having just spoken to Sean and both he and Marsha were in hysterics laughing. Sean had pulled up at the first farm he had seen and thought, this must be Jeff's place. It wasn't, it was some poor farmer's who was scratching his head wondering who the crazy dude was parked in his yard. Sean is lucky he didn't get shot! It made us both laugh and we moved on as quickly as we could. As it happens we didn't stop at Jeff's, I was in a pretty good place and ran quite well. Our target was to get to Chrisman on the border of Indiana where Marsha had arranged yet another free night's accommodation in a Bed and Breakfast called The Old Bick Inn.

Following Highway 36 through I eventually arrived in Chrisman at about nine p.m. where a small row blew up as Sean had forgotten to source food for that evening. There were no restaurants in the small town. All the hospitality had lulled Sean into a false sense of 'someone else will provide'. Well, there was no one else today, we had to find our own food. Falling back on our old failsafe, there was a petrol station that sold pizza. I had become accustomed to eating in petrol station forecourts (maybe this will explain to Zoë why I am reluctant to eat in a restaurant – I miss the smell of petrol).

After a pretty good pizza and my usual two litres of Dr Pepper – such a healthy diet – we headed off to find our B&B, which turned out to be a large, beautiful building in the heart of Chrisman. We were met at the door by a lady called Joy who, as we had come to expect in Illinois, was very welcoming. The rooms were beautiful and spacious and the best bit was we had separate rooms. After so long on the road you don't know what a luxury that is. Just to have space that is yours.

To be polite I went downstairs to speak with Joy to tell her about our journey and thank her for her hospitality. We talked about faith and how my Christian beliefs had helped me keep going. Joy told us of her personal journey and her Catholic faith. It was so good to hear someone's life being so positively supported by faith. Before we left after a great night's sleep and a fantastic breakfast she gave us a miraculous medal each and one for our children at home. They had been blessed in Medjugorje, in Bosnia, a small town where Our Lady appeared to a group of children in 1981 and is still appearing to some now in adulthood. The blessing for me was special and I still carry that miraculous medal with me today.

My faith in humanity was very much restored in Illinois. I saw so much good in people that I crossed the state line into Indiana with a heavy heart. I wanted to hang on to their kindness, I wanted to return to normality, but I would have to wait for a little while longer.

CHAPTER 15
Indiana

812.85 miles to go
Your past is not your future

"Hold on to your potatoes, Dr Jones!" As soon as I saw the Indiana state sign, that quote from *Raiders of the Lost Ark* was the first thing that came into my mind and it made me smile. It was one of the first movies I remember seeing with my dad at the ABC cinema in Belfast and ever since I have had a soft spot for Indiana Jones. Now, I know, apart from the name, the state of Indiana has nothing much to do with the movie but the significance for me was that I knew I still had my sense of humour. I hadn't cracked up completely. I was still able to laugh.

For long parts of my journey I seemed to have forgotten how to laugh. I did not have fun when I probably should have. I took things a little too seriously and I was determined not to allow the final three weeks to be too serious. I still had lots of running to do but I was going to try to enjoy it.

The first bit of fun was finding a covered bridge. I'm quietly a bit of a bridge geek. I like nothing better than studying the different and extraordinary lengths people go to, to cross rivers. It is something that we all take for granted but in the early days of travel and exploration a bridge could be the difference between life and death and I have always been fascinated by them. That is why I decided to start on the Golden

Gate Bridge and finish via the Brooklyn Bridge.

The covered bridge acted as a shelter to travellers caught out in a storm and served the communities as a place of safety. With 'Cross this bridge at a walk' written above the entrance and the date of 1876 I couldn't help but smile and wonder if the builder knew I was coming. To think that I was walking on the same bridge as the early pioneers of this great land brought a lump to my throat. All across America I had thought of the hardships endured by so many in those early days. Crossing the bridge connected me to the past. I knew my hardships were nothing in comparison to theirs, yet I drew great strength from that bridge, drawing on the souls from the past.

Indiana, however, was not going to let me daydream for long, the drivers on the first day seemed hell bent on killing me. Not intentionally of course, they were too busy texting on their mobiles to do it intentionally. I leapt four times into the ditch during the first hour – this was not a time to switch off mentally. As you can imagine I got a little annoyed as it appeared that all the drivers in Indiana texted whilst driving. I am sure that is not the case but I had come too far to get knocked over, my radar was on high alert.

Still, I enjoyed the challenge of the busier roads and was starting to enjoy the frequency of the towns. Montezuma and Rockville came quite quickly and although they were not heavily populated I got the sense that I was close to a big city. That big city was of course Indianapolis, which I was very excited about. I still had a few days to go but I was really looking forward it. We had managed to cross almost the entire USA without running through a really big city since leaving Sacramento at the start of the run. Our change of plan in Denver, Colorado, had meant we avoided any others in our way.

Another motivating factor about Indiana was that it is quite a small state. I had planned to take only five days to cross it and, psychologically, this would give me a big boost as some of the states seemed to go on forever! Five days was nothing. Getting my head down and powering through was the plan. Unfortunately, my feet had other ideas. The Adidas Boost trainers I had bought in Fort Morgan, Colorado, had served me well. They had certainly been a blessing. It was time to get a new pair. I had held off because of lack of funds; we could not really afford a new pair of shoes but it had got to the stage that if I didn't get a new pair I would put in doubt my ability to reach New York at all. We scraped enough money together and decided that once we found a running store in Indianapolis I would buy another pair. With around 600 miles left to go I figured that the new shoes would be the final pair I would need. What I didn't allow for was that Adidas had only just released the 'Boost' and that getting another pair would be nigh on next to impossible.

As I made my way into Avon, on the outskirts of Indianapolis, I was on the lookout for a running store. I was hoping for something along the lines of The Salt Lake Running Company in Salt Lake City (where else?) that gave me great service and advice. I was starting to lose hope when I caught sight of The Runners Forum tucked away in the middle of a large shopping plaza. I looked to the heavens and thanked the big man once more.

The store was amazing and on any other given day I would have spent hours trying on new trainers and probably spent hundreds of dollars. Today was not one of those days. "Have you got any Adidas Energy Boost?"

"No," was the simple reply from the lovely young lady serving us. "But we do have..."

"I want Adidas Energy Boost."

"Sorry sir we don't stock them but we do have..."

"I need Energy Boost," was my slightly crazed reply.

"I will gladly call some other stores in the area." I think she finally realised that I was a one type of shoe kinda guy! After several phone calls to different stores around the Indianapolis area we came up with nothing. The shoe was like rocking horse shit; typical, of all the shoes in all the land I had to choose the one that no one yet stocks! I sat despondent with my head in my hands thinking I can't face having to get used to another shoe. Taking pity of my obvious distress, the young lady then said, "Let me call the owner." The owner was great and quickly got on to their Adidas rep, Alex White. Alex was super quick to respond and sourced a pair of shoes about one hour's drive from us. What a lifesaver! We stocked up on hydration tablets and thanked the young lady for all her help. Sean headed off to get the new shoes and I plodded on through the heat, humidity and traffic systems of the city.

With Sean on a mission for a couple of hours I was pretty much on my own and I had to limit my water intake, as I had no idea how long it would take him to get back to me. The sat nav had said one hour but with big city traffic who knows? I just got my head down and powered through. I could see the city skyscrapers in the distance. It is always a wonderful sight to see the tall buildings of a city in the distance, they seem to draw you in. I have to say I thrive in the city, I am not a country boy! I couldn't wait to see what 'Indy' had to offer.

The traffic was unbelievable! So much noise and beeping of car horns. I loved it. The traffic junctions took an age to get across and as I ran through the traffic I got strange looks from the stressed-out commuters coming home from a hard day at the office. Suddenly, I realised that I had the greatest job in the world. Every now and then I would get a smile from a child in a car, I think in their world they knew that what I was doing was fun and that commuting in a car with stressed-out parents trying to negotiate the heavy traffic was not. "Come on Dad, let's run!" I imagined a child shouting from the back seat. Wouldn't it be awesome if we all stopped our cars and started to run home? Just a mass abandonment of the machine that so often seems to control our lives? My thoughts were running away from me, I was lost in my own little world.

Sean had been away for what seemed like an eternity. I had long since run out of water and although I passed many stores I didn't carry any money, so I couldn't buy any drinks. It was bloody warm and my body was screaming with cramp and hunger. I just kept hoping he would appear soon. It would, however, be another three hours before he was able to meet me and then he didn't have the ability to find the road I was on. Cities freaked Sean out, his brain when into 'lock down' and he couldn't work out the one-way system. After several failed attempts at a rendezvous we decided that he should wait outside the Capitol Building and I would find him. Frustrated and very hot, I was becoming badly dehydrated and very hungry.

When I finally made it into the city limits of Indianapolis it was fantastic. What a beautifully modern city. I ran past a huge Zoo (how I wanted a day off with my kids at the zoo) and I could also see the main football stadium and a baseball ground. This was definitely a big American city. I also enjoyed seeing lots of fellow runners out for their early evening run by the river. Due to the dreaded iPod I didn't get many nods or conversation but I know that everyone runs for a reason and it is usually to escape the hustle and bustle of the daily grind. What better way than to run by a river and blast the Prodigy into your ears? I get it! I would still have loved someone to join me for a few miles and to be able to share my journey with a fellow runner. I settled for a few "Hellos" from some pretty women and a couple of grunts from the passing men.

The energy I get from a big city is hard to explain but I almost felt revitalised as I ran toward the city centre. One of my favourite childhood memories was travelling into Belfast city centre with my mum or dad to go shopping on a Saturday. The streets were alive with people that seemed to move in a continuous wave. I loved the thrill of being in amongst so many people knowing that Belfast was my city, these were my people. I always arrived back in Glengormley, my home village, full of the excitement of the day.

Arriving at the city centre also made me feel quite emotional. It was a small success in the grand scheme of things, "Once we hit Indy we are almost home," I remember saying to Zoë before I left. Running beside the bustling businessmen and women I fought off the urge to shout, "I've just run here from San Francisco!" like some crazy person. Half of them just looked at me like I was crazy anyway, so I probably should have given it a go. Instead I quietly moved on to the Capitol and Sean.

When I finally found Sean he was busy; not sorting out food or hotels, no, he was taking pictures like a bloody tourist. I was hungry and thirsty and he didn't seem to care. When I asked him where we were staying that night he told me he didn't know. It was already past six p.m. so he was leaving it late to find something, "I've been busy finding your trainers," was all I got. Boom! I totally over-reacted and chewed the face off him. I ranted about the fact that he had not cared I hadn't had a drink for nearly three hours or eaten since lunchtime. All he was interested in was taking fucking pictures of the city hall. We were here to do a job not fuck about acting like tourists!

I put on my new trainers, which, by the way were bloody awesome, and stormed off, leaving Sean not knowing which way I was going or where the next rendezvous point would be. I was so furious I didn't care – he would just have to figure it out for himself. It is amazing what a little bit of anger can do especially when added to a new pair of trainers. I was opening up my stride and almost running at 10k pace... for about two miles. After which I was absolutely knackered. The stress of the day had finally caught up with me. I had also reached a part of town that looked a little bit like a scene from the TV show 'The Wire'. I had seen drug dealers on street corners earlier in the day but these guys looked a little more menacing as the night drew in. There was also a lot more ladies hanging around on the street corners. It was time to end the day's running and get the hell out of there. That's if I could get hold of Sean. I was grateful that he hadn't sulked for long, and we ended the night eating the largest petrol station pepperoni pizza ever. After 36 miles it tasted pretty awesome.

Our motels all seemed to be much the same across the States but I do remember being a little scared in Indy due to the amount of fights that broke out amongst the residents. As time went on we found out that motels are used as short-term housing solution for families. Great for them but not much good for the weary traveller who has to listen to the inevitable domestic arguments that break out when people are forced to live in a small space. We were also awoken by someone trying to get into our room and testing the strength of our car door handles outside – it was a pretty awful night's sleep.

In the morning we did our usual McDonald's breakfast and headed back to where we had ended the run the night before. Hopefully, the drug dealers and prostitutes had gone home. Tired and a little confused Sean managed to drive through a red light. Fortunately, we did not crash. Unfortunately, he did it right in front of a police car. I looked in the rear view mirror to see the flashing lights of a police car coming up behind us. Oblivious to the red light, Sean was a little confused as to why we were being pulled over and when the officer asked him why he hadn't stopped at the signal Sean's response was incomprehensible. Not that he was trying to be obstructive but until Sean has drunk two litres of Seven Eleven coffee he cannot speak to anyone in the morning. The officer looked across at me as if to say, "Seriously? What the fuck did he say?" I explained that we had genuinely not seen the lights and that we were new to the area. He looked into the back of the car to see all our gear and asked the inevitable question, "What are you guys up to?" I explained that I was running across America raising awareness of recovery from addiction and his whole demeanour changed. He gave a little smile of admiration and said, "I am going to have to make a call."

Sean was shitting himself by this stage. In his head 'making a call' meant that he was going to be handcuffed and carted away... I could almost hear the cogs of his tired, coffee-free mind turning. When the officer got through on his phone his conversation made things a lot clearer. "I have two guys on a traffic stop and one of them is running across the USA to raise awareness of addiction recovery, do you guys want to run a story on them? Yeah, I have them stopped so I can keep them here until you get a camera crew down." He had rung the local TV station; we had been stopped for running a red light and were going to end up on TV! What a result. We waited for 20 minutes and sure enough the TV crew turned up and did an interview with us.

I not sure the interview made it on to TV but it was a pretty cool thing for the officer to do for us. We thanked him for all his support and thanked him again for not giving us a ticket for running the red light. He shook our hand and warned us of the dangers ahead and gave me a further, interesting piece of advice, "Remember prostitutes with all their teeth are usually undercover cops." Laughing, we set out on the road again.

The Adidas rep, Alex White, who had helped locate my new trainers, called me that day. I had left a message to thank him and let him know that the new shoes were awesome, so, when he called back I was expecting it just to be a courtesy call. Alex explained that when he first received the call he thought I was just some spoilt tourist and he hadn't really shown that much interest in what I was doing. That changed when he logged on to our Run4Sobriety website. He and his wife were staggered by what I was doing and wanted to show support by joining me for a few miles running at the weekend. Wow! I was stoked for a number of reasons. Firstly, that he had taken the time to look at our website and fully appreciate the challenge I was undertaking and, secondly, that he was willing to give up some time during the weekend to come and run with me. I was over the moon at the prospect of having a running buddy for a few miles.

Our route had now taken us back on to the historic Highway 40, the route that had taken early settlers west, that I was following back east, and I loved being on that road. The spirit of the travellers I have mentioned before was growing stronger. The towns going out from Indy became smaller and had a hardworking feel to them. Back in open, rolling fields and fresh clean air made running so much easier. The temperature dipped below 30 degrees, which also meant I was more comfortable. I also felt a little safer running into the evening. On my way into Knightstown there was a police stop in progress right in front of me. As I approached I could see that there were children in the car and that their father was being arrested. A second police vehicle pulled up with what I presume was a police sniffer dog searching for drugs. It really upset me as the children were still in the car obviously upset at the flashing lights and confusion around them. In fact, as I write this I can't help but cry thinking of the future those kids have in front of them. I hope they find the strength to break the cycle. I ran past unable to offer support or an answer. I just said a prayer for their parents to seek a better future.

Prayer is something that became almost second nature on the road. I would often drift off in prayer for people in my life. In fact if you are reading this and have known me for a while the chances are I prayed at some stage during the run for you and your family. I hope you don't mind?

The churches along the route would have quotes and sayings on the notice board outside and one of my favourites was 'Prayer is the best wireless connection'.

On my way into Richmond on the Ohio state line I had had a pretty tough but enjoyable day. Highway 40 had taken me through Dublin(which Irishman wouldn't get a lift from that?) and also through Cambridge (I always knew I would make it to Cambridge one day) and I had been boosted by all the monuments and plaques about heroic tales of travel and politics giving the area a great sense of adventure. As the heat had made it hard going all day I was pretty tired and wanted to finish early but I was determined to get past Richmond to give myself a chance of being in Ohio on Saturday morning. This would put me back on target. As I ran towards the outskirts of the town I was approached by a man standing at the side of the road. My first reaction is always to clench my fist ready for action (it's an Irish thing) but thankfully this meeting was not going to be anything like I could have imagined.

"Hey man, why are you running?" was the first question.

"What makes you think I'm not just out for a leisurely jog?" was my initial response, "Why do you ask?" I added.

"I saw you running past my house earlier and, as I prayed after dinner God told me I had to come and see you. I have been standing here waiting for you, as I knew I had to speak to you. I just want to know what you are running for." Completely amazed, I told him about Run4Sobriety and he realised why he had been told to speak with me. He had recently lost family members from drug addiction and was struggling to come to terms with it. Maybe meeting me was a way for God to give him strength to spread the message of sobriety in his work as a youth minister. We both knew it was a special moment. We prayed together at the side of the road and shared a moment of clarity.

Your past is not your future and your future has not yet passed.

I moved on up the road full of the Holy Spirit. I genuinely think that the encounter I had just had was one of the most spiritual moments of my life. Often I have read of people having moments of vision and clarity at times in their lives when they are feeling most vulnerable. I was certainly feeling that way. I am sure some psychologist would be able to explain it better but I think the vulnerability allows you to accept what's in your heart and see beyond what is directly in front of you.

I relived the story to Sean when I arrived in Richmond. He too was a little freaked out by the encounter and we decided to retreat to the motel and be thankful to God for all our blessings. Not before we hit McDonald's though!

CHAPTER 16

Ohio

576.8 miles to go
Running friends

We had been texting Alex all day whilst we made our way toward Richmond. The plan was that I should have made it to Ohio by Friday night but the events of the previous evening had left me about a mile short of the state line. We agreed to meet up with Alex and his lovely wife Brianne in our motel car park and it must have thrown them a little when they called us that morning to find us eating breakfast in, yes you guessed it, McDonald's. "These guys can't be running across the States eating McDonald's?!" I can imagine them saying.

We quickly finished our pancakes and syrup and made our way back to our motel. It was great to actually meet Alex after speaking to him over the phone. I instantly liked how he rolled. He genuinely looked so enthusiastic to meet us and he was already dressed ready to run! Before we started he went into his car and pulled out an Adidas bag filled with running gear: t-shirts, shorts, tracksuit tops – it was like a runner's Christmas, best of all for me was another pair of new Adidas Energy Boost trainers. I now had the luxury of being able to rotate my shoes. You would be amazed how much more comfortable the last seven hundred miles had been with decent shoes.

We set out on the road. Alex told his wife Brianne that we would do ten or so miles and then they could spend the afternoon together – I wonder if she actually believed that?

Alex got his first taste of life on the road as we navigated over a busy intersection and were nearly run down by the trucks and cars heading for the interstate. He also was there to witness me crossing over the state line. It was strange sharing a moment like that with someone other than Sean who had driven ahead because it was too busy to stop. Sean had been with me at every state line, mind you I was glad Alex was with me. We took the obligatory state line photo and continued up Highway 40.

The route quite quickly became rural as we ran past fields dotted with farmsteads. Matching our rhythm, this was a great opportunity to get to know all about Alex and to tell him about our journey so far. Obviously, working for Adidas he was super interested in all things running but he also loved all sports and it was great to listen to him talk. It was so good to be out on the road and have someone at my side. Since Catherine left in Utah I had done every mile on my own. With Alex my running also improved, partly, I suspect, this was down to good old macho manliness and not wanting to let Alex see how I was suffering. I knew he could run and I didn't want to embarrass myself. When I think back I really had nothing to be embarrassed about as I had run from San Francisco for fuck's sake! I really should have eased up on myself.

The challenge of having another runner was great for me though, as it showed that my fitness levels were pretty high. I was able to hold pace for every six-mile checkpoint. At the second checkpoint we decided to stop for something to eat. This was where Alex had intended to end his morning out with us but he made the inevitable phone call to Brianne to say he was going to do a 'few more miles'. I suspect by this stage Brianne knew what that meant. Lunch for Alex was a few healthy nuts and an energy gel; for me it was a couple of slices of petrol station pizza. I had passed the stage where I worried about food, I just went for the most calorific and probably horrific thing I could, as it seemed to be working for me. Lunch always kick-started my day. The afternoons and evening were still the best times for me to put in good mileage.

That afternoon we came across a group of Native Americans who were also crossing the continent. They were travelling from east to west and their run was called Return to Alcatraz and we stopped and chatted with the guys for about 20 minutes. They explained their reasons for crossing the land. They were walking to support indigenous people and nations that are carrying on the struggle of affirming indigenous sovereignty: stopping exploitation of land, protecting and maintaining traditional spiritual belief and protecting sacred sites. They were doing it as a relay, so when they heard I was doing it on my own they were suitably impressed. I was just glad to finally meet some Native Americans. One of the observations both Sean and I made throughout our journey was that there was little or no mention about the influence and impact of the Native American inhabitants. Often the only reference to their existence was the commemoration of a massacre or village raid. I have great respect for these guys staying true to their roots and showing immense pride in their heritage. Something we can all learn from.

That day was almost perfect conditions to have a running partner. The road was straight, the weather was not too warm and the sky was a beautiful deep blue all day. Funny, how vividly I can recall that day above all others. Brianne finally relinquished all thoughts of having Alex back before dark at about four in the afternoon when she arrange for us to go for dinner in a lovely little Italian restaurant in Englewood. Sean felt out of place eating in a restaurant, but we just enjoyed filling our face with yet more carbohydrates! Sitting all together gave us more time to get to know Brianne a little. Having spent all day with Alex I could tell these two were a perfect match for each other. Brianne is a very caring individual and had the same warmth and interest in our journey as Alex had. I really enjoyed chatting with her and to be honest could have quite happily stayed there all evening eating and talking but Alex had that look in his eye, that look that says, "I want to run an Ultra!" Up until that day Alex had only ever run a marathon. Having said that, he had done a pretty fast marathon if my memory serves me right (around three hours) but he had never ventured into my world, well, I was happy to take him there. So we finished dinner and drove back to the last checkpoint and took him into 'ultra world'. The last ten miles were pretty perfect miles with great straight roads and beautiful scenery. The only thing going against us was the failing light. I was happy to run into the night on my own but I was a little less happy about putting someone else's life in danger just for a few extra miles. We had a quick chat and agreed on a target figure of 36 miles, which was pretty awesome for Alex's first ultra. It also saw us finish just about nightfall in the car park of an ice cream parlour. A perfect way to finish a perfect day! My journey was made richer that day for meeting both Alex and Brianne and I don't think Alex will ever fully understand how important his gesture to run with me was. He stood tall that day with a fellow runner, he stood tall with a struggling brother.

FB post 12 August 2013 Alex White
Glad I could help out a bit!

The next morning was so strange setting off to run on my own. I found myself looking to my left to chat to someone. It was back to solitary confinement. It never took me long to get into that mindset and I think that that ability was probably a major factor in the success of the run up until that point, I was happy with the solitude. I have always felt isolated and alone, struggling with identity issues and confidence, even now the solitude of writing this book takes me to a place where I feel safe.

Now I was heading for Columbus which was another large city. I hadn't seen a city for so long and then two come along at once! First, I had to make my way through Springfield, Ohio. Ah Springfield, probably the worst town I encountered in the whole journey. Traffic was always dangerous but there was also always a certain level of respect; often drivers would wave or beep their horn in appreciation. Not in Springfield, all I got was abuse or gestures to get off the road. This in turn made me become a little bit antagonistic back, I waved at every goddam car I could and this seemed to drive some of them crazy. We have since found out that Springfield, Ohio, is one of the most depressing places to live in America. I can confirm that. Chill out guys!

Leaving Springfield to grapple with its own issues, my memories of heading into Columbus was of anger. Yet again I had to run through some of the most deprived areas I have ever seen with drug dealers openly pushing on the streets. I had tried to ignore this issue, as I know we have the same problems in parts of the UK, but there was something about the area surrounding Columbus that got to me. How could the police not be dealing with this obvious criminality? How can any child grow up in these neighbourhoods and feel that they can succeed in life? The sight of the large banks and law firms in their hi-tech skyscrapers profiting in full view of other people's misery was hard to take. I don't want any American readers to take offence at this, as I feel the same way when I travel into London, but the gap between those that have everything and those that have nothing is SO wide I may have to run that as my next challenge. I quickly regained my composure and remembered that being angry solves very little. I was running for a different reason and I needed to get on with it.

As a city Columbus was one of my favourites. I think that may have been influenced by the fact it is named after a great explorer and fellow adventurer. Now, obviously I am not comparing myself to the great Christopher Columbus, but in a small way I too am on a quest for change and discovery, although mine is a personal discovery and his was an entire continent! The fact that I was able to have any association with such a great explorer was a great boost to my morale. I was entering the last two weeks of the journey and now daily had to fight against my mind telling me I'd done enough. Obviously I had not done enough as I was still in Ohio but my brain had other ideas. Any energy I could draw from a city statue or monument was a great help in the last two weeks. I enjoyed taking my photo of Columbus and hitting the road for the last few miles of the night with his adventurous spirit inside me. I didn't stay adventurous for too long though, as I started to enter a neighbourhood that had some very dodgy characters. When a young man got aggressive after I refused his request for money and then his request for my credit card, I knew it was time to hit our motel, which turned out to be a lot like our experience in Indianapolis: people trying car door handles and fighting in the corridors until three a.m. didn't make for a great night's sleep. No sleep the night before usually meant a tough next day. I was still managing to get in the mileage but the fatigue and pain I was now in was indescribable.

Although my new shoes had made the run more comfortable I don't want you to thinking I was pain free. I wasn't. The pounding my feet had taken would mean that Nike, Adidas and any other shoe manufacturer would have to ask God himself for a solution to what I was feeling. The pain in my feet was only matched by the pain in every other part of my body: my knee was now so sore I had given up even trying to find a solution; my hips ached so badly that simply lying on my front would cause me to cry out in pain; my shoulders were solid with tension and I was in dire need of a massage. In fact my entire body was wracked from the thousands of steps I had taken since leaving the Golden Gate Bridge. I had no choice but to take some painkillers and, at the end of every day, wait for a small window of pain-free sleep.

The west side of Columbus was a totally different experience to the east. I ran past multi-million dollar homes for most of the morning in the leafy suburbs. I tried not to get too annoyed but it kind of justified my feelings the previous night. I think I had to remember that one man's good fortune should not be envied – just spread the wealth a little brother.

I was pretty pleased to start making my way back into the countryside now. I was on the edge of the Appalachian mountains, so the terrain had become a lot hillier than previously. I didn't mind it to be honest, as it was such a beautiful place to run. Having crossed the Sierra Nevada, the Uinta and the Rocky Mountains I felt at home in the hills. The trees and the wildlife had become my companions, the hills like my big brothers. I felt safe. I also had in the back of my mind that I was only two weeks away from going home. Two weeks from finishing this unbelievable journey. The thought of crossing the Appalachians had worried me but after everything I had been through I knew that I could cross them without them slowing me down – I couldn't afford any holdups now.

Along my route the Amish communities became more frequent but despite a couple of hellos there was little other interaction between us. I did witness a buggy race on a back road just outside of Zanesville where two young lads had decided to test each other's manliness by having a race. It was great to see healthy and slightly dangerous competition between two young men. Us men are all the same really when you cut away all the nonsense.

One evening we were set up to stay in a small place called Cambridge where Sean had managed to find a pretty decent motel at a decent rate. We discovered long ago that the closer you are to the interstate the more expensive the motels become. I was pretty pleased with a good strong 40-mile day and was settling nicely into my dinner when my mobile phone rang. This was quite unusual as Zoë and I usually spoke during the day. The only other regular call I got was from Stevie Walker and I had already spoken to him.

"Hi, is that Tom?" said a voice with an American accent.

"Yes it is, who is this?" I replied quite abruptly as my McDonald's was going cold, "Hi Tom, this is Tony Culley Foster the only other mad Irishman to have run across the USA." Wow, this was phenomenal. Tony was indeed the first Irishman to have run across America in 1976. I had a brief email conversation with him before I left but we were both so busy it didn't lead to anything. Unknown to me Zoë had contacted Tony in a bid to boost my spirits for the last push. Boy, did it work. I am immensely proud to be an Irishman but since leaving Ireland in 1986 the Irish media tend to disinherit you but I can assure you the years of living in the UK have taught me that I am not and never will be British. I am Irish and proud. So to be able to speak to the first ever Irishman to complete the journey meant I was honoured and he knew what I was going through. We talked for about 30 minutes about what I had seen and encountered and he told me how he had dealt with certain situations. He was also keen to point out how I would feel when I had finished but I think I chose to ignore that part as I wasn't there yet. He was right about one thing though, my life would be changed forever. We agreed to speak again over the coming days and said goodbye. My head was all over the place with the emotion of the conversation. Despite the 40 miles run that day and the fact I was in so much pain I was nowhere near able to sleep. It was going to be a difficult night.

The closer I ran to the finish line, the more used I became to my disturbed nights. They usually involved me going over and over all I had been through and then playing through different scenarios of how my life would be when I got home. I would spend hours perfecting a speech to give at the town hall in Wakefield because surely the City of Wakefield would honour me? How wrong I would be! (My local paper didn't even bother to send a journalist to see me, they wrote an inaccurate story and ran it on page 37 of the paper. This really does piss me off even now. Most cities celebrate the achievements of their residents but it appears Wakefield is only interested if you are involved in Rugby League.) I would then spend the rest of the night playing motivational videos from You Tube to gain inspiration for the next day. By the time I had done all this it would be around three a.m., the painkillers would have kicked in and I would finally fall to sleep, only to wake up at six-thirty for another day of pain. That was pretty much the pattern for the next 12 days until the finish.

The section between Old Washington and Morristown became a little trickier as Highway 40 turned into Interstate 70 and I was forced to use the back roads and these really were back roads. They led me into some beautiful hills but most were gravel roads that played havoc with my feet and I seemed to spend an eternity pulling stones out of my shoes. The scenery really was spectacular though. As I rose higher and higher into the hills I could look out over what seemed to me to be the whole of Ohio. The farmhouses were easily visible in the sweep of the landscape, each having a large grain silo and the traditional red barn beside it. There is something familiar, even iconic about these red barns. I suppose it is the image we know from the movies and they are quite beautiful, especially when viewed from on high looking out over the entire state. Psychologically though, it drove me crazy as none of the roads were straight. I had been used to moving east almost constantly since leaving Colorado, but these roads took me north and south and it felt like I was making very little progress. When we got to a section that was closed off completely I went nuts. It added about three miles onto the day which could have been worse but it still pissed me off sufficiently to have a few swear words to the big man upstairs. As the night drew in it got a little scary. Previously I had always run on open highway but on these small roads lined with trees I got the creeps, it felt like I was the unwitting victim of a horror movie. I did not run for too long into the night as, to be honest, I am a big girl when it comes to that! Give me a chick flick over a horror movie any day.

I calculated that I had one more day in Ohio and was determined to hit the state line of West Virginia. Thankfully the temperatures in Ohio had dropped and I was managing to get in an average of 36 miles, sometimes 40. The difference running in 20 degrees compared to an average 35 was remarkable. I actually felt fit for those last few days in Ohio. Judging by some of the hills I was encountering I was going to need to be. The Appalachians were finally upon us.

I had moved well that day and was finally accepting that night time running was inevitable if I was ever going to make New York on time. Being able to run faster was a big help, it also gave me more time to recover in the evening before finishing the day strong. I was still in lots of pain but I was in a good place.

As I approached the town of Wheeling I knew that all I had to do was cross the river and I had made it out of Ohio. It was dark and the suburbs were not the best but I was determined to push for the bridge. I had to get out of Ohio to give myself a mental boost, the boost that says "That's another state done Tom". I arrived in Wheeling, West Virginia, around 10.30 p.m. I was exhausted and excited all at once. Sean knew we had made significant progress over the previous few days and was starting to believe that we could actually make it.

CHAPTER 17
West Virginia

421.4 miles to go
Car trouble

To keep the direction of the book on track I suppose I must write a little about West Virginia. Initially, I was hoping to skirt around the top of the state as it was messing with my head a little to think I had yet another state to run through. On the flip side I also knew that even though it was another state I would be through it in less than a day. So, psychologically, it was going to be more beneficial to run the state. Also, our route naturally guided us to the sharp tip of West Virginia and really left us no other choice. Sean also had mentioned earlier in the trip how cool it would be to go through it as he liked the John Denver song 'Take me home, country roads', which, when I think back, was a pretty appropriate song for the journey.

I hadn't taken much notice of the town of Wheeling the night before as it was at the end of a 39-mile day and, to be honest, I was pretty shattered. Setting off through the town the next morning you could tell it had a tough working-class edge to it. I got a sense that this town would have acted as a gateway to the west in the early settler days. In fact for a bridge enthusiast like me it was like being in heaven. The Wheeling Suspension Bridge was the first long span suspension bridge built in the US in 1854 and lessons were learned from it that helped the design and construction of the Brooklyn Bridge in New York, my final destination. It felt good crossing the Ohio River knowing that I was now within touching distance of New York but, irritatingly, our car did not feel the same way. Shortly after setting off that morning, in fact just as I crossed the suspension bridge, Sean told me the bad news that the car had broken down. Apart from a flat battery and a couple of flat tyres we had been lucky really and had no car troubles, now with only ten days left to go it had decided to call it a day. Sean had already called for roadside assistance and I trusted him completely to get it sorted. He had become quite resourceful over the last month, in fact, the change in Sean was remarkable. He still couldn't get out of bed on a morning but he had started to think a little more. He had finally become proactive rather than re-active. He seemed to have lots of things under control although I did detect some frustration about this happening so close to reaching New York and I felt it too. We could have driven to New York from Wheeling in a day, but we still had ten days of running left. We almost had to go back to our original strategy, which was not mention New York, at all, I had a lot of running to do yet and I could not let thoughts of home upset me now.

Leaving Sean to deal with the car I filled up early for what could have been a longer stint without support. I was determined not to be caught out like I had been in Indianapolis and I was pretty glad I did as the climb out of Wheeling was quite severe. These early hills were a taste of what was to come, yet, I liked this part of the journey. As I made my way out of the town the suburbs began to take on a more historic look. I was now getting to the part of America that had some history (history from before the 1840s that is). The expansion west took a long time and the discovery of gold, before it really took off. This area though had been settled for a decent amount of time, the historical plaques were now listing dates in the 1700s. Now, for us in Europe this is not that long ago in history terms, our history is well documented back to and before the Roman invasion, but I liked the fact that I was getting closer to the well-established East Coast.

The route through West Virginia was pretty straightforward. I had to go through one small town interestingly called Triadelphia, which, apart from a small garage and a barber shop had not much else going for it. Sean did manage to get his hair cut though and this time it was much better that the cut he got from Dick in Utah! He also, we hoped, managed to get the broken car fixed. We crossed our fingers and pushed on. My thoughts throughout the day were simply to get out of West Virginia and into Pennsylvania. So, that's what I did, I got my head down and smashed through the mileage, always moving east.

Chapter 18
Pennsylvania

384.4 miles to go
I love them goddamn hills!

I arrived in Pennsylvania late afternoon on the same day I left Wheeling. It was a pretty low-key affair. Unlike all the other states there was no state sign welcoming me, just a small marker indicating I had entered a new state. It seemed such a shame, as this was a pretty momentous moment for Sean and me. This was the last big state. New Jersey would only take me two and a half days to cross, so this was the final big test, it was me versus the Appalachian Mountains.

I had been running in the foothills of the Appalachians in West Virginia and there had already been some big climbs. Not like Colorado, where the mountains rise up to 9,500 feet over five miles. The Appalachians rise 2,000 feet in the space of a half a mile – these bad boys are steep! Coming out of Wheeling I had hit one climb and to be honest I quite enjoyed it, as the downhill stretch was lovely and this was what was going to make the Appalachians different; the steep climbs and descents. With my new shoes I felt my feet cope with the downhill and I was able to make great progress. The scenery, however, was not something I was prepared for.

My journey so far had taken me to places so beautiful I never thought they could be bettered. The calmness of the Sierra Nevada with its pine forests and the limpid Lake Tahoe; Nevada's tough solitude surrounded and filled by the rugged beauty of the Great Basin; Colorado gave me The Rockies and in return they asked for nothing apart from me to appreciate the true beauty of God's creation and Kansas showed me the way to feed a nation using the great open plains of the Mid West. I thought I was all out of appreciation by the time I left West Virginia until I reached the Appalachians. It's just the most beautiful place I've ever seen, that's the only way to describe it. I don't think I can do it justice, I'm sure painters could not fail to produce a masterpiece from the landscape, even writing about it now I am brought to tears at its simple beauty. There is no singular iconic landmark it is just the way it has aged so beautifully, apparently untouched by human hand. No obvious signs of settlement just mountain sides carpeted in trees, lush valleys, crystal rivers and fields.

I knew I was going to like this state.

The problem I faced was that, despite the beauty of my surroundings, I had mentally switched off. I had around 300 miles left to go and I knew that I was almost finished. My brain was getting busy sending my body signals saying, "We are nearly finished!" and anyone who has ever done an endurance event will know that once your body starts to give up on you it's very difficult to get it back. Every mile on that first day was as difficult as I can remember. The only way round it was to trick my busy mind with a little reverse psychology. I told myself that I was nearly finished so the last few miles should be easy. I convinced myself I was in no pain and that I was a finely tuned machine with energy to burn. This lasted for about five miles. The fact was it was not all mental. I was in pain, extreme pain. My knee injury was finally taking its toll on me. It was a constant aching of the joint, it never went away, even when I went to sleep I had to protect it with pillows to make sure I didn't knock it during the few hours' sleep I actually managed every night.

As I knew already there really was no chance of me not finishing this event I needed to man up a little and in my own words, "Embrace the pain!" This was a bit hard after 90 days of embracing the pain, but there was nothing else to be done.

That first day we arrived in the town of Washington. It was late evening by the time we reached the outskirts and as I approached our agreed meeting point I saw a police car pulling up. I was about a half mile away from reaching the stop, which meant Sean had at least five minutes on his own with Pennsylvania's finest. After the Indianapolis incident I didn't really trust Sean to talk to this guy and not get us locked up! I upped the pace a little. When I finally got to the car you could see the look of relief on Sean's face. He had been telling the cop about our journey, but in the absence of a runner the cop remained unconvinced. Until I showed up. I asked him what the problem was... "Californian plates." What the F**K? The lady owner of the house that Sean had parked outside had phoned the police because she was suspicious of our Californian licence plate. Now, I'm not sure what I find more alarming, the fact that she called the police, or the fact that the police came out. If you called the police in the UK about a man parking his car outside your house and asked them to attend they would say, "Is the man trying to kill you? No? Then why are you calling us?"

I presumed that once I had given him our story he would shake our hand and let us carry on. Only he didn't, he asked for ID and visas so that he could verify what we said. Even though I knew we had done nothing wrong I have a 'guilty' button that makes me convince myself I'm going to jail and I had already planned my defence in the five minutes it took for him to run checks on us. I almost put my hands out and said, "It's a fair cop governor". Thankfully, he apologised for taking up our time but explained that Californian plates so far east arouse suspicion from everyone. The woman must have thought we were on a drug run! No harm, no foul so we were on our way.

I enjoyed the fact that Washington was a busy place after the country roads of the daytime, it allowed me to run quite late into the night. As I made my way through the town I came across a Life Church, the same as the church I go to at home. I smiled as I remembered the time spent with my family in church the previous year and how it had really made us stronger as a unit. Having that connection with home allowed me to finish strongly and I felt content that night.

With Highway 40 having now having turned into a busy interstate, I was back on the country roads, with all the advantages and disadvantages that brought. The main advantage was a quieter road, the disadvantages were they were far less direct and the traffic we did encounter was usually not prepared to see a runner on the road. This made things a little more dangerous, especially around some of the corners and I relied a lot on sound. I had become quite good at hearing vehicles coming along the road too fast. My senses where definitely heightened throughout this stage, the last thing I wanted was to be hit by a truck so close to the end. Mercifully, I had no real worries as my skills at avoiding these situations were now well honed. I had become a road traffic ninja, skilfully negotiating my way between cars and trucks and leaping for cover with spilt second accuracy. I've mentioned it before but nerve wracking as it could sometimes be, I enjoyed the battle to be honest – it kept things interesting and as I moved through each town the traffic dropped any way.

With the exception of my night time terrors, I enjoyed the solitude of running the country roads. The hills on the other hand, not so much. Some of the areas toward Monongahela were just beautiful places to live. Monongahela itself was an old town on the banks of a river. Founded in 1769 you could tell it was steeped in history and I have since found out that Joe Montana, the NFL hall of famer, grew up there, and it is now its big claim to fame. This small town of less than five thousand people produced one of the best quarterbacks in the game of American football – well he had to come from somewhere.

I quite liked the town but I liked it more because the McDonald's had a great Wi-Fi connection and I was able to speak to my son Niall via Skype. I loved being able to keep contact with the children. I missed them all so much.

Spurred on by the great chat with Niall and then Zoë, Orla and Oliver, we crossed over yet another huge river aptly named the Monongahela River and I headed on to pick up Highway 31. This would take me all the way to Bedford. I liked these long stretches on the same road, I didn't have to think or look at maps, just run and eat.

The first big test of the Appalachians was on this road in the shape of Laurel Summit, which, compared to the mountains in the Rockies, was small at 2,728 feet but, as I've already mentioned, it was a steep climb. I got a great sense of achievement getting to the top. I had missed the hills, I'd had no significant climbs since Cameron Pass in the Rockies, which I was thankful for but it is always nice to run in the mountains. The air was fresh and the wind was cooling, it was a welcome break from permanent heat and humidity. Being at the top of a mountain gives me a sense of worth and, then, a great downhill section which, despite my knee, I really enjoyed and even though my feet were smashed to bits they were not quite as sore as the first 2,000 miles. I was able to run quite strongly for long periods before having to take pain relief, I was keeping up the mileage and even walking up the steep sections, I was hitting my target of 36 miles on most days.

After another late day on the road we arrived in Somerset, even the place names were telling us we were getting closer to home.

Before I got to our motel I got some extra mileage in up Highway 281, as this would take us to the Highway 30 and give me a better start in the morning. On the route I noticed a sign for the Flight 93 National Memorial. I hadn't realised that our route would be going past it and it was quite a sobering thought. Even though I had suffered on my journey it served to remind me that others have suffered far more and their loved ones continue to suffer the effects of 11th September 2001. Sean and I agreed to visit the site the next morning.

On the last mile of the night I went past two guys having a yard sale. I could tell to look at them that they had both been drinking heavily and by the way they were talking they probably had taken a few illegal substances too. I stopped to chat, as it had been a long day solitary day, but as soon as you speak to a drunk American man and the word Vietnam is mentioned you know it's going to get tricky, you also know that he will have a story to tell and that he will have forgotten more pain and anguish than you know. If you listen closely enough and get past the crazy you will gain a real insight into his life. Long story short, after I told them what I was doing both men basically admitted they had drink and drug problems. One of them remarked that, "They had so many reasons to drink and none not to." Looking in their eyes I believed that. These were troubled men. Even though they could probably have done me some real harm, had it suited them, I felt comfortable around them. I felt they accepted the things they could not change but embraced the fact that I was trying to change the things I could. We chatted for about 20 minutes and I said my goodbyes. Their parting advice to me was simple – if any drivers give you any shit shoot them. I laughed and quickly began to run!

That night we had booked into a Super 8 motel at the side of the interstate. We had decided to take a break from our usual McDonald's and try an Arbies. This was just another shit burger chain but it made a change. As always we had our food before I showered, so walking into a burger joint after 36 miles on the road meant I looked a bit of a state. When we arrived there was hardly anyone in the place but as soon as we placed our order two separate groups came in behind us. The first group were what I would describe as college kids and the second group appeared to be musicians. The first group were white the second black. As we sat down the comments started flying from the college kids about me looking like Forrest Gump, although not to my face. I don't mind a bit of banter but I got the impression these comments were supposed to get me upset. They then turned their attention to the set of musicians and although I didn't hear any direct comments the tone of their conversation was about how much they hated black people. Sean could detect that I was getting into fight mode. After 36 miles I was ready to take these guys out! To my surprise the group of musicians appeared to just laugh off the comments that they obviously heard and left the restaurant with their heads held high. They had made the college kids look like idiots by not rising to their words. This was a great lesson for me. I unclenched my fist and ate my burger.

The next morning I actually thought I was in Somerset, England. The rain came down from about four a.m. and didn't stop. Normally in the UK rain would never stop me running but I had run over 90 days and, with the exception of one afternoon in Kansas, I had managed to stay dry. I had come too far to get wet now! I insisted that we see if it eased up a little. I used the safety argument to make sure Sean didn't think I was getting soft but in all honesty I didn't like the thought of getting piss wet through. It was hard enough getting the mileage in when the sun was out, it would have been soul destroying to have to do 36 miles soaking wet. It wouldn't have been safe anyway (ahem, still trying to justify it), the spray on the roads would have made visibility poor and left me quite vulnerable.

We therefore settled into an extended breakfast and got chatting to some bikers who had also wimped out from riding their Harleys in the rain. They made us feel like celebrities asking for photographs etc. it was a lovely way to spend the morning. Finally, as it must, the rain eased off just after 9:30 a.m. and we were on the road again. Running towards Highway 30 en route to the National Memorial.

The loss of life that day in September 2001 was so horrific; watching it unfold on the TV, the stranded and desperate people, the images of those that chose to jump and then the inevitable crashing to the ground of both towers is something that will stay with me forever. I had then visited Ground Zero on a trip to New York with Zoë and had found the whole experience quite traumatic and emotionally draining. Having had that experience I was quite worried about visiting the site of Flight 93 (if you don't know about Flight 93 you should!) yet, since it was on our route we could not justify avoiding it. Even after our late start we could not go past without stopping and paying our respects.

I met Sean at the gates and we drove in. We had no idea what to expect. The car park was busy but not full. I tried to tidy myself up but I still looked like a crazy bearded hobo. The mood was almost funereal, children fell silent, eye contact was almost at a minimum and heads were lowered in reverence to the bravery of those involved. The usual brashness of the American tourist was not to be seen here. The actual impact site is about a mile or so off the highway and as we walked towards the memorial I got the distinct impression that I was getting some strange looks. Did they think I was a Muslim? Is that what they were thinking? Was I being paranoid? As I sat down in front of the memorial the people that had just sat down instantly got up and gave me a look of disgust. Normally, I would have asked what their problem was but I figured that this was not the place. I asked Sean if he thought I was being paranoid and he said, "No, I think it's time we left". There were no comments made and I hope it was our paranoid minds but we did leave quite quickly after paying our respects. Despite our experience I came away feeling pleased we had made the time to visit. Having spent the previous three months getting to know America we had a better understanding of the patriots on that plane, normal men and women who took charge of the situation and sacrificed their own lives to save other Americans. We had met these good people all the way across the states and I for one was glad to call them my friends. RIP Flight 93.

The route along Highway 30 was as straight a road as I'd seen since leaving Nevada. It was to take me up another mountain, this time with the very funny name of Bald Knob Summit. I'm not sure if this translates to the same thing in the US but in the UK if you call anything a knob it always gets a chuckle. It also reminded me of a story that Steve in Illinois told me about a time when he was travelling in the UK. He bought an antique door handle from a store in London but he couldn't understand why everyone laughed when he asked to put the door handle into his wife's bum bag. "All I said was 'Tiffany can I put my knob in your fanny?"' and everyone laughed at me!" The use of English words is so different and can get you in a lot of trouble.

The summit itself was quite spooky. It was deathly silent for a while as fog swirled around the top, but my anxiety was calmed when a large oil tanker screamed past me far too fast for my liking and headed off down the hill, brakes screeching and breaking the eerie silence. Going down the other side I got a glimpse into the past of the Highway 30 before the interstate took over. I came across the site of an old hotel called the Grand View Point. It was situated on a sharp bend about half a mile from Bald Knob Summit and the views overlooking Pennsylvania were absolutely spectacular. I can imagine the hotel would have been a great place to visit in its heyday. It boasted a view of three states and seven different counties. I had images of old cars all polished up for the weekend away, children drinking from cold coca cola bottles, eating fruit pie and having ice cream and the ladies all dressed up living the American dream. So sad to see it is now just a parking bay. I do hope some entrepreneur decides to resurrect the old place. But with no time for sentimental meanderings my job was to get down the mountain. I had actually felt cold up there, the first time I'd felt cold since Echo Summit in California, mind you, I didn't stay cold for long because as soon as I came down from the top of the mountain the heat picked up again. I didn't mind the heat at this stage; it was below the magical 35 degrees which I now had a tolerance to. I remembered back to California when if it rose above 20 degrees I was in real trouble, could I be actually starting to enjoy the heat?!

The route and view down off the mountain was stunning. Winding roads that took the view away from you only to give it back a mile later with a, "Wow, look at that!" I even managed to convince myself that if I squinted and tilted my head to the left I could see New York. Of course I couldn't, but it gave me a boost to pretend. The mood between Sean and me was also pretty good as we both enjoyed the fabulous landscape. Although that could all change at a moment's notice. He was in a pretty good place apart from a slight detachment from the whole journey. I think Sean had also told himself that we had finished, so there were times when he needed a kick up the arse to get him motivated. Despite appearances, we were both on a knife edge and at any given moment our mood could change.

This happened at the back end of the day for me. Despite having had a great time climbing over Bald Knob Summit and enjoying the stunning views my mood started to slip. I fell back into an 'I don't want to be here' slump. Now, this probably feels like self-pity and I can hear some saying, "Just snap out of it Tom, you're nearly there!" but it was not a conscious thing, it is just the way I felt and I was past trying to understand why I felt like that, although it probably had something to do with the 2,800 miles of running and nearly four months away from home. Either way these feelings usually passed after a few hours. I was pleased when I finally arrived in Bedford where we stayed at Judy's motel.

Judy's was a classic American motel. I'm sure you can probably tell I hadn't been over impressed by most of the motels we had stayed in but this was still family-owned and run. There was a certain homely feel to it and they looked after us well. I didn't venture out that evening for dinner, instead I asked Sean to bring some food to the room. After a tough day I wanted to hide away.

I was feeling a lot brighter the next morning and instead of hitting a subway or McDonald's we decided to find a proper café. There was no better way of starting the day than a good feed of bacon, eggs, hash browns and pancakes. Bedford was quite a town. Very old and, I suspect, quite middle class, it still had rails to tie your horse to and they really knew how to cook a breakfast – I was stuffed! I really enjoyed the morning's running too, as it had occurred to me that I had only seven days left on the road. One week and I was done. I reflected on how I had been over the previous month. I'd been hard on myself and so determined to succeed that at times I had forgotten to enjoy it. On the flip side of that I was proud of the fact I wasn't patting myself on the back for what effectively was achieving nothing. I still believed that anything short of

New York was a failure. The last seven days were going to be enjoyable, I knew I could do it in the time left, even if I had to walk 36 miles a day!

Climbing out of Breezewood over another mountain range I was moving at a decent rate for what seemed like an eternity. When I finally lifted my head, yet again I could see all of Pennsylvania laid out before me. I was reminded of seeing a sports psychologist just before I did the Marathon des Sables back in 2010. I had been having issues with quitting races at the slightest little thing going wrong; slipping and falling or having to tie my shoelace during a race would result in me throwing a tantrum and walking off the course. I obviously could not afford to do that during the MdS, as it wasn't the sort of race you could walk home from even if you wanted to. Plus, it had cost over three thousand pounds to enter. Anyway, this sports psychologist was not really the answer but she did give me a bit of advice that was worth the ridiculous sum of money she charged me. She told me to look up! That was it! However, if you think about it, it's a quality bit of advice. Many of us go through life working so hard on one thing that we forget to take time to raise our heads to look in the direction we are going. We arrive at a point in our lives without having noticed what's passing us by or even what's right in front of us. Some of us find ourselves in a nice place but that is purely by luck. Too many of us find ourselves doing a job we don't like, living a life we don't enjoy with people we don't care for. So, it's really important to look up, look around and see where you are heading, look around at who you are, who you want to take with you and, most importantly, look to see what you have achieved.

As I looked around I could see what I had achieved. Not only that morning's climb but also, for as far as I could see, where I had run from. I was pretty happy with that, I was going to look up more often.

Our original plan was to head to Chambersburg and then up to Carlisle but there was a good advantage going a little off track towards Fannetsburg. Sadly, this meant that any hope of a trip to Gettysburg had been dashed. Of all the places in the States I would like to see Gettysburg is it. To be so close and not be able to reach it was quite frustrating but once again we reminded ourselves that we were not tourists, this was not a vacation.

The route was very simple and had the advantage of taking us parallel to the mountains and also move us further north. We needed to start moving north as New York was slightly above our current position. As I ran on I was treated to another full moon that night, which always kept me in good spirits. There is nothing better than running into the night with the moon shining a light on you.

Back tracking a little to find a place to stay, Sean flew by the seat of his pants for dinner and managed to find a restaurant in Fannetsburg, well, when I say restaurant it was a table at the back of a general store. It did serve pretty good pizza though and that night we drove back to a motel near the turnpike. It had been yet another tough day, especially the last few miles, as I had to cut across some hills to join the road at Fannetsburg. We had less than a week to go...

The motel we stayed in was pretty poor and had no signs of any breakfast facilities so we trawled the Internet to find a café. I was drawn to K's Place which was quite a distance, taking us back further towards McConnellsburg. Sean was a little put out at the thought of having to drive back down the road we came in on just for breakfast but I just had a feeling about the place, I had to go there.

When we arrived it was a nice simple place, quite busy with a good mixture of people. We sat down and the lovely waitress came over to us. She instantly identified us as British and laughed when I insisted we were, in fact Irish. We got chatting and as usual she was astounded by what we were doing. I had become accustomed to people saying, "That's awesome!" That's not me being big headed it's just that it had become normal (and it was pretty awesome). She focused on the addiction side of things quite quickly and asked why we had chosen addiction. I told her my story as she sat down beside us, "You really need to speak to our newspaper editor. I will call him now." As she picked up the phone she also said, "You also need to speak to the owner." She didn't say why but I could sense there was something wrong.

We had a great breakfast and chatted on the phone to a local newspaper editor. It was all good fun and there was a great atmosphere in the place, but I needed to know why the waitress had said I should talk to the owner. I eventually got her to sit down and tell me what had happened. The owner's son had been a drug user and, sadly, had over-dosed only a matter of weeks earlier. At the age of 47 he had died leaving four children. There was a silence from both Sean and me. The reasons we had been guided here were making themselves known. She went on to tell us how the owner had also lost his wife only a few months earlier (though not drug related). This man had suffered unimaginable loss and I was almost lost for words. The waitress was insistent that we should go into the kitchen and speak to him. I instantly had a feeling of this is what our journey is for and made my way to the kitchen.

I spoke with the man quite honestly and I could see the obvious pain in his face. He looked like a man with no soul; his eyes were empty and his face emotionless. He then heard our story, of the journey we had been on and the hope we had given people. I told him that his son had done nothing wrong, he succumbed to an illness that kills millions, that the children should still be proud of their dad, that he should still be proud of his son, that the community cannot judge him, that we are all in this together as one addiction family. His face filled with colour, his eyes were no longer empty as they filled with tears and his mouth moved into a smile. We embrace and prayed. I thanked God for guiding me to that place, we prayed for a safe journey to heaven for the man's son and for his children to know they are children of God and that they will always be loved. We embraced again and left.

Sean and I didn't speak. We both knew something had happened that we could not explain.

I enjoyed the next few miles in a tranquil peace. The sky was blue, the wind was light and the scenery was beautiful. It was exactly what I needed after my encounter in the café. But there was a storm brewing in my head. The longer the day went on the angrier I became. After all we had done crossing this great country we had only really scratched the surface on the work that needed doing with addiction. The story of the café owner was being played out across all 51 states in America. It was happening in the UK and the rest of Europe. What was it all about? My run couldn't help save any of these lives. Why was I not a doctor or better still in government, someone who could really influence the lives of those affected by alcoholism and drug addiction? I ran and cried. I was in a pretty emotional state when it suddenly dawned on me, I was making a difference. The realisation came from the silence of my surroundings and the sound of the two sobriety chips deep in my pocket given to me by Jan and Carey so many miles ago. They had put their faith in me and I had given them hope. They knew that someone was on their side. The little jingling sound of the two coins had been drowned out over the past few hundred miles and although checking the coins was something I did every morning and night I would often forget about them. Maybe it was just a bit of luck being in such a quiet place after the meeting in the café or maybe it was a sign from God to remind me that my journey was blessed. Either way the rage in my heart subsided.

We were now heading for Carlisle through a series of small towns with definite European links, Roxbury and Newburg to name a couple. These were nice areas to run through and were a nice distance apart, allowing us to get supplies etc. Almost every town had a burger joint so Sean and I were happy. The only thing they didn't have was a motel. This meant driving further into Carlisle to get somewhere to sleep. It wasn't a massive drive but it was a little inconvenient. We always opted for a Motel 6 if we could find one, as they were usually cheap and clean. The one we found in Carlisle was huge. We parked up and Sean booked us in. When he came back to the car disaster struck, the car battery was flat yet again. This was a bloody nightmare. We only had a few days left and we could do without this nonsense and it had only just been repaired a few days earlier. I went to the room and left Sean to sort it out. We also had the problem that the motel was so big we had to carry all the bags about half a mile to the room!

Eventually the decision was made by our car hire company to exchange our car. I was a little annoyed at this, as it meant clearing everything out of the car at past midnight. While I tried to rest I left the job to Sean and I should have known better. Not taking time to check he forgot to take out at least half our stuff, things we had collected or been given as gifts that we'll never see again, but that's Sean.

The upside was that we had a brand new car for the last few days of the run. It was quite a nice car too. I had hoped that we could now move on from the California plates and have possibly New York plates. Not us, this bloody car had Florida plates. I don't know which is worse, looking like a couple of drug dealers from Cali or looking like 'a couple' from the sunshine state.

Carlisle was a fairly big city. As the name suggests it has a British connection and it was almost like being in the UK, apart from the sunshine, with lots of red brick terraced buildings, and the college there is fantastic.

Dickinson College is, I believe, a law school but having seen their sports complex I think it's safe to say they produce one or two athletes. This is the kind of America we see on TV: very hot college students walking around looking uber cool with other, just as cool business people sitting out having lunch. Yes, this was the place to be. There was also a lot of military history to this town. It played a big part in the American Revolution and its proximity to Gettysburg obviously attached it to the Civil War. These are all things I love but sadly had no time to explore further.

I tried desperately to strike up a couple of conversations but most people gave me a wide berth thinking I was a crazy man. I suppose I may have looked OK in Carlisle, Cumbria but not Carlisle, Pennsylvania.

In no time I found I was out of the city and making my way towards Harrisburg.

The route toward Harrisburg also took in a couple of other 'burgs', including Mechanicsburg, a small industrial town about eight miles away from Harrisburg. A cyclist passed me on the road and I had had a small acknowledgement of my existence. I'd had several rants about how rude some lycra-clad cyclists could be. This is a worldwide problem I think. Some cyclists think they are better than everyone else once they put on their carefully chosen lycra suit; once they mount their £2,500 carbon fibre frame that weighs less than their wallet but offers no advantage as they are four stone too heavy, they become ignorant fools. Now, note how I say 'some'. Remember Hope in Kansas? But she was a fellow traveller of the road not 'weekend bike warriors'. Anyway rant over, this guy barely acknowledged me as he passed. About 20 minutes later he passed me again, this time going my way and stopped just up ahead of me. We struck up a conversation and I quickly realised that we had very similar backgrounds. We had both used exercise as a stress buster and loved being out on the road having different adventures. My initial annoyance at him ignoring me disappeared, as a matter of fact he probably didn't see me the first time as he went past so quickly. I enjoyed having the company of a fellow athlete for those few minutes. We keep in touch via email from time to time and it's good to know he's doing well.

Twitter 20 August 2013 @RayZahab
@dryingout dude keep rocking out there!!!

The run also began to take me through some very affluent areas. It was the American dream kind of place. Lots of very big houses and nice shops, there was a very different vibe about this place. I actually saw other runners out on the streets. It was very rare I ever came across another runner and I was enjoying the cooler evening air. It had been a pretty warm day so as the cooler night drew in I was able to up the pace a little. We had decided that we would try to get past the city limits by 10 p.m. We hit the city at about 6.30 p.m. It was a wonderful sight and crossing the inky black Susquehanna River I was treated to bridge heaven. Several bridges had been built over the river. It was quite a sight in the early evening sun. Again the city did not disappoint and as I made my way through the streets I marvelled at the buildings and the wealth, as I had done in almost every city. But, every city has its bad parts as I had witnessed. For some reason I had let my guard down as the run into town was so beautiful and I presumed that this town would be different. Wrong! As I crossed the road into a new neighbourhood I saw the police detaining someone in a car, the young men being dragged out and handcuffed. As I passed I thought it wise to ask some advice from one of the cops. "Is this a bad area to be running through?" I asked.

"Yeah man it's bad."

"How bad?"

"Dead bad, man you're not wise going up through there." I am glad I had asked the question. It turned out that the area was one of the toughest I'd encountered. The officer directed me through some streets and told me I'd be safer there but not to run too late into the night. The streets he guided me through left me a little uneasy. This really was a tough neighbourhood. Thankfully, I eventually made it on to a busy road and continued to make good progress. I had called Sean to tell him to be on his guard. After which I am sure he was sitting in the car with his doors locked.

I had my head down making my way up a hill on my new route when I could hear someone running up behind me. After the conversation I'd just had with the police officer I was too scared to look over my shoulder to see who was coming. As the footsteps got closer I began to clench my fist ready for the inevitable punch up that would soon follow. I had come too far to go down without a fight. The person was just about on top of me, so I quickly turned to face my would-be attacker and saw a young black man was running as hard as he could towards me. I unclenched my fist, this guy was doing hill repeats as part of his training! I nearly died laughing. He ran about 10 metres past me and came back down the hill again. I stopped him and asked him what he was training for. "I'm joining the US Marine Corps Sir." Wow! I smiled and we talked about my journey. He was so respectful and kept calling me sir. Despite his surroundings he told me he was determined to get out of the poverty that surrounded him and make a good life for him and his family. I respected that. I asked him how many hill reps he had done. "Ten sir," and I then asked him how many he had left to do, "No more sir, I'm done," came the reply.

I asked him again, "How many have you left to do?" I smiled as I said it.

"One more time sir!" he shook my hand, smiled and headed off to do one more rep!

As I moved onwards towards Allentown I was getting that sense that the end was near, my daily mileage was 36 to 40 miles per day, but the temperature was on the rise. Forty-degree days was not what I had planned or hoped for. There was a feeling though that nothing could stop us; could I dare start to really believe that I would make it? Still the battles with negativity stifled happier emotions. As I remember and write, the next part of this book was a real struggle to get down. Zoë was instrumental in everything successful about the trip. So I don't want this to be a negative for her but to be true to the book and our journey I have to write about it.

I had a conversation with Zoë early morning and we discussed my return to the UK. I do not recall the whole conversation but the gist of it led me to believe that despite having been away for four months the only person that appeared to have changed was me. Everything we had discussed before I left that Zoë had planned to do remained undone. All the personal change that had been promised to me had not happened. Now, I want to make this clear, in normal circumstances this would not be an issue. I love Zoë, I love everything about her and everything she does and has done for me before during and after the journey. In my shattered mind, however, struggling with loneliness, pain and bone-deep fatigue this manifested itself as a major deal. I had convinced myself that upon my triumphant return my family would be perfect. Zoë would be fit and healthy, the house would be freshly decorated and the children would be speaking fluent French or whatever other thing I'd convinced myself would be a valuable addition to my 'new' world. The conversation with Zoë shattered my world. There was no new lady to return to all fit and athletic. The house was in the same state as when I had left and the only language the kids had learned was Yorkshire. I got angry and upset and did my usual act of sulking for the rest of the day. I never move well when I am carrying a burden. Looking back I hate the fact that I had let my mind become so fragile that I put that pressure on Zoë. She had looked after the house, cared for the kids, updated the event website, worried over our finances (or lack of them) whilst holding down a job and fretting about me. She was Wonder Woman and all I had done was shout at her. I seriously had to sit down and get things in perspective. That evening, as we arrive in Allentown not far from the state line I got a grip of myself and remembered that the journey was not about us changing as a family. We didn't need to change. My little tribe are pretty tight, we are a solid unit.

FB post 24 August 2013 Angie Haring
What Tom is doing to raise awareness for sobriety is awesome. I wish I had the stamina to join him on his fight. I wish him well on his sixth year of sobriety and am glad I had the chance to meet him and his brother

The final day in Pennsylvania was pretty special. The route was taking me through the town of Bethlehem. I don't know what I was expecting but it was just a lovely town with a peaceful vibe. Bethlehem has such meaning and not just for Christians. It is a symbol of a journey against the odds to make it to a safe place. A symbol of a new beginning. Being a Sunday morning the local Catholic church was very busy. I almost wish I'd had the confidence to go into the church to pray and to speak to those in the congregation. I wanted to grab their attention. I didn't. I just ran past and hoped I would get a quick acknowledgement. I didn't.

Pushing on, the route towards the state line was simply beautiful. The peacefulness of the mountains, the clean air and the countryside calmed me, I had straightened myself out, Zoë and I were friends again. As I headed into Easton I was able to breathe a sigh of relief that I had made it over my final mountain range. That was my final test. The New Jersey state line was within touching distance, it was all that stood between me and New York City. It was kind of fitting (and to my delight) that the New Jersey state line was on another fantastic bridge. It was as though the bridges of the United States of America were built for me. As I stood at the halfway point on the bridge I knew I had made it. I had arrived at the start of my final state...

CHAPTER 19
New Jersey

91 miles to go
Julian

It was always tough when I arrived in a new state late in the afternoon. The temptation was to say, "That's it I've done enough," but in reality I hadn't done what I needed. If I wanted to make sure I had an easier day on the last day I needed to get a 40-mile day in. It was hot though, very hot!

After suffering in the late afternoon sun, by chance we stumbled upon an ice cream parlour. I always stopped and had ice cream wherever possible, it was an instant pick-me-up and the memory of Sean bringing me an ice cream in Utah had stayed with me. As we sat eating a quite delicious mint choc chip ice cream in what little shade the car park offered, Sean and I decided to use the time to update social media on our progress.

"RIP Chalky."

This was the status update that I read on a friend's Facebook post. There is only one man that goes by the name of Chalky in Wakefield and that was my long-time friend Julian Charles.

"Are you talking about Julian?" I commented.

"Yes," was the almost instant reply. How can this be happening? No, it can't be Julian no, please no! Was all that was going through my head.

Almost instantly my timeline was filling up with status updates: "RIP Chalky".

I turned to Sean as he too was picking up the same messages. Confused, I called home and spoke to Zoë. She too had heard.

This can't be fucking happening I cried out! Julian can't die! I was so far from home all I wanted to do was be able to speak to someone who knew him. I called Stevie Walker who also knew and he explained that he didn't want to tell me until I had finished the day. I understood. But he was gone; my good friend was gone.

Julian was the first friend I ever made in England. We met in Snapethorpe hospital where we played football on the hospital field. I don't remember how the friendship started, we were just young lads happy to find a good mate and since then he had always been in my life. He was not my constant companion but when we saw each other he always greeted me like a brother. In our teen years we would see each other in the bars and nightclubs of Wakefield. He would always take the piss out of my accent no matter how many people were around. In our 20s we went our separate ways but always enjoyed bumping into each other and catching up. We would talk of the past and our plans for the future. He was always a larger than life character especially as he was literally a giant of a man, but however tall, his character, was not his size but his heart.

He was a great brother to Marquis and Rachael and I know that as an uncle he was idolised. Julian was a true one off – there was no one like the 'big guy', there was only one Chalky.

Back out on the road I felt stunned. My mind was all over the place. When you lose someone like that so far away from home all you want to do is be with your loved ones. I spoke to Zoë at great length about how I was feeling and as always she knew what to say. "Julian would want you to finish." Throughout our journey we had been dedicating days to sponsors and to people with special events or celebrations, at no stage did I ever think that I was going to have to dedicate mileage to a lost friend, but that's what I did. We dedicated the remainder of the day to Julian's memory. I would love to say it eased the pain in my heart but it didn't. I plodded through the remainder of the day and I was pleased when it was over. I finished that day at 11p.m. I was emotionally and physically exhausted but happy that I was only two days away from New York.

Whilst I was concentrating on putting one foot in front of the other, poor Sean was battling with the motel from hell. He had found a motel on the route, which was great, as a long drive to the next available place late at night was not that appealing; however, the woman on reception more or less accused him of trying to use a fraudulent credit card to pay for the room. Her reason was we didn't have a name on the card. It was in fact the name of our non-profit making event website and was all above board. We had used it in 97 places so far across America, yet this lady decided we were frauds. When I heard I was furious, but Sean simply did what he now did superbly and left the motel to find another without any fuss.

As I tried to understand the events of the day I sat and watched music videos on YouTube. There was one I had been particularly fond of the previous night. I had played it over and over. The song was by U2, 'Sometimes You Can't Make It on Your Own' I heard the lyric speaking to me, "Listen to me now, I need to let you know, you don't have to go it alone..." I felt as though it was telling me when I returned home that my solitude was over, that I could start to let more people into my life, that I had to accept that my life was too tough to try and make it on my own. Writing this chapter I am listening to the words again but this time I hear them differently. I now hear them as a message from Julian. The song was played at his funeral and I can't help thinking, playing the song as I did the night before he died, that it was a signal – that he was with me on my journey. That he will always be on my journey. There are people that come and go in our lives but, as long as you want them, they can remain forever in your life through their spirit. Julian's spirit is everywhere I go.

RIP brother.

Shattered and emotional I thankfully managed to sleep well because we had an early start. Just before the sad event of the previous day we had made arrangements with Sophie Power to pick her up in Newark. Sophie was a friend from the Marathon des Sables race. She was in my tent and we shared experiences that only MdS race veterans could understand. She had contacted me in the early days of my run and had said that she was planning to be in New York around the finish date and would I mind if she joined me? It was a huge honour that she would even think about joining me for the run.

That conversation had been so long ago that I had almost forgotten she had offered until she contacted me about a week from the finish. She would be in New York and would be available on the second to last day of my run. I was so excited at having Sophie join me. She is the most positive and lovely lady I have ever met. Her timing was perfect, as I needed support.

Sean headed off at 6 a.m. to pick her up from Newark train station and I was dropped on Schooleys Mountain on the way. It broke my routine a little as I hadn't had time for my early morning ritual toilet time. As I ran through the beautiful country roads of New Jersey I began to realise I was going to need to find a bathroom; I also began to realise this just as I got into a more built-up area. Just my luck – 99 days on the road and I was in danger of crapping myself 50 miles from the finish! I was also thinking of the surprise Sophie would get when she arrived. Thankfully, I made it to a very posh sandwich shop in Chester. I must have looked quite desperate when I ran into the shop. They looked as though I was robbing them. I suppose having a bearded man with a back pack running into your store could be quite frightening but doubly so when the bearded man has the look of "I need a shit now!" on his face. Trouble was they didn't have a fucking toilet! NOOOOO! I asked an older man outside the shop if there were any public toilets. No public toilets, but there was

a 'porta john' on a nearby construction site. Yes a thunderbox came to my
rescue. I have detested 'portaloos' all my working life having spent many
cold winter mornings on building sites all over Yorkshire suffering the
temporary toilet hell! I almost kissed this one. It was a small luxury and
certainly beat the alternative.

I returned to the café with a different demeanour and had myself a
very relaxing breakfast. The ladies behind the counter still didn't know
what to make of me but at least I had lost that look on my face.

Sophie arrived around 9 a.m. It was so good to see her. She was also
ready to run with a no messing around, 'let's get straight out on the road'
attitude. The difference in my running that morning was unbelievable. I
felt strong and I had around 40 miles to do before I hit the outskirts of
New York. I had done six miles before Sophie had arrived and I could tell
that she had no intentions of letting me slacken off the pace. I told Sophie
of the previous days, troubles and she almost took that as a sign that we
needed to run strong for my friend. We seemed to talk constantly from the
moment she arrived, that's the ultra-runner mentality to talk as we run. At
least it used to be when I first started. Lately, I've felt it has become a little
too competitive for me. Most of my recent good friendships have been
born during long arduous runs. Jamile Siddique and George Henderson
to name a couple are friends that I knew nothing about before I ran 90
and 60 miles respectfully with them during ultra-running events.

Sophie has such a beautiful view of the world that I could listen to her
for hours. We are from very different worlds. She is a very well educated
and well-spoken young lady. I suppose if it were not for ultra-running
our paths would not have crossed. She did a great job of breaking down
any barriers of class and education by just being pretty cool.

We decided to sit down for lunch as we had made such great time.
When we met Sean outside the agreed meeting place he didn't look
pleased; after all the miles we had travelled and the cities we had navigated
he had managed to get himself a parking fine. I couldn't believe it. On
our 99th day we get a ticket. He had parked facing into the traffic, which

in America is illegal and they were very quick to spot him. I was a little annoyed but it was near the end so I didn't lose my cool. Zoë, on the other hand, went crazy. She knew exactly how much we had left in the account for the last few days and we certainly could not afford a parking fine. We had next to nothing left. Our finances had always been tight and thanks to the generosity of our sponsors we had managed to get so far but it was very tight though. We really could not afford any more slip-ups or we would be sleeping on the streets until our flight home.

We had to take this one on the chin and I didn't let it spoil lunch. We sat and chatted about the journey and allowed ourselves a pat on the back. It was becoming real now. Signs for New York were becoming more frequent and I convinced myself I could already see that iconic skyline.

Sophie ran with me until 3 p.m. after covering close to 30 miles. Sean then took her back to Newark. Having Sophie there that day was exactly what I needed after losing Julian on Sunday and she will probably never know how much she helped me. Her words along with her actions will remain with me forever. Thank you, Sophie.

Sean headed off and I was allowed to have what I felt was a relaxing end of day run. I basked in the glory of my hard work that day. I was proud of my effort running with Sophie and was happy that she had run so far with me. This was my time now though. I made my way through the suburbs of Newark wanting to shout to everyone about what I had done. Some of the suburbs, however, didn't look ready to give me any sort of reception. These were tough neighbourhoods but they were exactly the neighbourhoods I needed, full of energy and noise. I'd had my quiet reflective time when I could gather my thoughts, this was a time for adrenaline and emotion. I was always full of emotion and up to this point I had done my best to hold it in. As I ran down through the streets of Newark I was smiling so much my face ached. My tears of joy hidden by my ever-present sunglasses and there was a spring in my step that said I had finished. As I got closer to Newark city centre I started to feel happy. I had promised myself to try and enjoy the week leading up to the finish but with Julian's death it hadn't happened but I needed to enjoy and savour these moments.

I met up with Sean on one of Newark's main streets. He was surrounded by street sellers and with his typical British niceness he had managed to strike up a conversation with the toughest dude on the street. What he had failed to notice was that while he was chatting his 'associates' were eyeing up our car. As I approached from a distance I could see what was about to unfold. I engaged the guys briefly before whispering in Sean's ear what was happening. He quickly switched his brain back on and jumped in the car and moved it to a safer location, as I talked to the street sellers. Now parked safely we hid in our final McDonald's of the journey.

We had spent so much time in these places they felt safe. Almost a second home. I am not promoting a life of sanctuary in McDonald's by any stretch of the imagination but it is amazing how a fast food outlet can almost be a safe haven for travellers around the world. We enjoyed our burger and relaxed as we only had three miles left until we hit the bridges that would lead us into Jersey and then over the Hudson River onto our last checkpoint of the day.

The final three miles that day I ran in the gathering dusk. The evening air was still very humid and I was beginning to stiffen up after the day's efforts. We didn't care though as we were enjoying the atmosphere of the place (me probably more than Sean, as he had to sit in the car in some pretty dodgy areas of Newark). It was a nice feeling getting to the start of the bridge network. I decided I wouldn't risk any more in the dark. I had done enough and it was time for one last motel before we hit New York City.

FB Post 23 August 2013 Scott Bailey
Tom, you've achieved something quite heroic! Thank you for sharing your adventure with us. Thank you for showing us what is possible in life. Thank you for showing people you can live a full and meaningful life without alcohol or whatever addiction holds you back.

Chapter 20

New York

16 miles to go
Where dreams come true

FB post 27 August 2013
FINAL DAY
6 years ago Tom told me he would get sober, I had faith in him.
In October Tom told me he was going to run across America. I had
faith in him.
Today Tom is 6 years sober and will have run across America.
Faith is a wonderful thing.
All my love Zoë x

I awoke on the morning of August 27th 2013 with a feeling of relief. You'd be forgiven for thinking that I was relieved to have made it to New York, but that wasn't it. I was relieved because I had made it to six years sober.

Twitter 27 August 2013 @ClonesCyclone
@dryingout Good on you Tom, many congratulations.

August 27th is my date of sobriety. I planned my run so that I would be in New York on that date. I thought it would be the best way to show those struggling with addiction just how far you can go once you leave the booze behind. I had no idea when I first decided to give up drinking that my life was heading in this direction. In fact, one of the biggest stumbling blocks for me to stop drinking was the fear that my life would get worse, not better. My warped logic being that my life was already shit and alcohol was the only thing that made it bearable. Yet, here I was six years to the day since I made that decision, sitting in a motel room with Sean having just run across the United States of America. Whatever I thought six years ago it wasn't this. I was happy just to have a day, a week or even a month sober. I had no idea people actually did stuff like this back then.

I reflected on the events of the past 14 weeks and then on the past six years. My life had changed immeasurably and I felt proud. What also occurred to me was that I had actually succeeded in something that others thought impossible. I had finally succeeded at something in my life. Some might say what about the marathons you have run like the Marathon des Sables? Yes, those were good but this, this was great. This one really took me to hell and back and I survived. This proved to me that anyone suffering from addiction can get their lives back on track, and not just get it back but really excel in whatever they want to do.

Going down to breakfast that feeling of relief had quickly turned to nerves. I struggled to eat anything but knew that I had to get something down. As we sat watching others move about the restaurant completely unaware of our epic journey we simply smiled. We did not feel the need for conversation.

FB Post 27 August 2013 BreakingTheCycles.com
You've travelled an amazing journey together, Zoë and Tom, and together shown us what courage, strength, hope and recovery can do... Thank you.

We drove to the start point, which looked very different than it had the night before; the traffic was certainly a lot busier. We took a moment to get our thoughts together and I said a prayer. I thanked Sean for everything he had done. He was the only man that could have done the job. No other person would have coped with my demands for so long. I told him to always remember the struggle we had to get to this point. It would make our lives so much easier in the future. We had a brotherly embrace and took some photographs and then I set off.

As I made my way over the bridge on Hudson Bay I could see the Empire State building and the rest of the hard-edged New York skyline. The skyscrapers take over the view. It is an image that is already in our sub-conscious due to our love affair with movies and American TV shows. At the edge of this great land is a city that beats all cities and this is it. New York. The first time you see it, it smacks you in the face saying, "I own you!" As I looked across from that bridge I screamed out loud, "I've done it, I've fucking done it!" and the tears began to fall. All the issues and the struggles had been about that moment. The sacrifices made not only by me but also Sean, Zoë and the children. Their sacrifices made this possible.

Making my way through Jersey I knew I was heading into big city traffic. Everyone was totally focused on negotiating their stretch of road. I did get a few waves though, as I made my way through the bustling streets toward the Holland Tunnel.

 FB post 27 August 2013 Michelle Gregory Congratulations Tom! You did it! I am so glad I got to meet you along the way.

The day was warm, 28 degrees. It was strange that I hadn't noticed that. I was sure I would suffer for it later but I was enjoying myself. The road network was a little difficult to navigate but we managed to find a way through and as I ran and walked I caught up on social media messages. The response had been fantastic. Messages from people that had been following the journey from day one were the best. They spoke as though their favourite TV show was about to finish. I hadn't realised the impact my journey had had on some people's lives, Zoë was updating my mile-to-mile progress – I loved the fact that people were following the last day 'live' as it happened from New York.

 FB post 23 August 2015 Lizzie Hastings Thank God x

The only thing bugging me at the back of my mind was Stevie Walker, an amazing supporter of my effort, Stevie had called me almost every day to check on my progress and he hadn't called that day. I remember saying to Sean, "That little bastard has let me down! I need his support today." Sean told me not to let it bother me as no doubt he would call at some stage throughout the day. I was pretty pissed off. How could he not have known I needed him today?

FB post 27 August Alex Flynn
You did it! So amazing and proud to know you mate! Knew you could make the distance. Well done!

I had spoken to Zoë several times throughout the morning. She and the children had made a beautiful video for me with Orla singing 'New York' a song by Jay-Z with Oliver doing the beats. Knowing that they had spent so much time doing the video was so special to me. I had missed them all so much I was finally allowing myself to show that emotion. I missed my children every single day but I think, even more, I missed being able to feel emotions of love that I had had to keep a lid on for 14 weeks. Zoë had been with me on every step of the journey and at no stage did she falter. I am sure there were times when she could have said, "This is enough I want you home," but she stayed strong. Even on the day when Oliver ripped his ear off playing in the garden she coped with it brilliantly. He required stitches to a nasty cut but neither Oliver or Zoë asked me to come home. This is the kind of unwavering support my family have always shown me. Zoë asks for nothing yet gives me everything. She played an integral role in the success of this trip and I wanted her to enjoy the last day as much as me and I called her from every landmark. When we arrived at the Holland Tunnel ready to make our way across the Hudson River I called to say we were almost there. She sounded so excited.

FB post 27 August 2013 Nick Eklöf
Still can't get my head around what you've actually done. Credit to you! Unbelievable!

Not open to pedestrians (or trans-continental ultra-marathon runners), we had to drive through the tunnel and emerged on the other side in Lower Manhattan. I had finally arrived in the city of New York. The concrete jungle. I jumped out of the car and agreed to meet Sean at the Brooklyn Bridge. The sounds all around me were electrifying: car horns blared, people shouting, people running, I almost blended into the crowd of crazy New Yorkers. The heat of the day kept the exhaust fumes low in the canyon-like streets, so it was hard to breathe at first then the city boy kicked in, I took a deep breath and remembered this was my place, this was my time.

I had really wanted to finish on the Brooklyn Bridge but Zoë's instructions were that I had to make it to Coney Island. The Atlantic Ocean was the finish and, as we know, Zoë was the brains of the operation and she was of course right. This was a coast to coast run.

 FB post 27 August 2013 Mike Gibbs
Well done big lad! An amazing personal achievement!!!!

Before I reached the Brooklyn Bridge I took a small detour past Ground Zero. When I had visited some years ago the site was still a construction zone and had a palpable feeling of sadness around it. I spent most of my time there remembering back to that horrible day and was filled with deep sorrow. This time it was different. Freedom Tower was almost complete and the area around Ground Zero had a different feel. It was a feeling of hope, of renewal and recovery. How fitting was it to be in a city that had been brought to its knees and almost destroyed by an evil act. This city could have chosen to give up, to let outside forces destroy it. It chose to recover. It chose to get off its knees and fight for its right to be here. It struggled and stumbled along the way and the healing process is far from complete but New York showed us that recovery is possible from anything. I was proud that day to stand and have my picture taken at Freedom Tower. Stand up New York and take a bow. I salute you.

From Freedom Tower my next stop was the mighty Brooklyn Bridge. I had been so excited about seeing this bridge (I had missed it on my last visit as Zoë, inexplicably, does not share the same appreciation for bridges that I do). I had managed to run down the wrong street and entered the bridge from a stairwell about 50 yards from the main pedestrian entrance. I rang Sean to ask him where he was. He told me I had to get to the pedestrian entrance because that was where he was. Fuck that! I thought I was almost at the towers of the bridge at this stage. "Why can't you come to me?" I said, he just laughed and told me to get to the start of the bridge. What was he up to?

As I approached the bottom of the bridge I noticed that Sean was talking to a few men. Who was he talking to? Then I noticed the all too familiar figure of my good friend Stevie Walker – so that's why he didn't call! As I ran towards him I also noticed Steve Gage, another old friend from Wakefield. I couldn't believe that these two had flown up from their homes in Florida to welcome me to New York. Both Stevie and Steve had made the move from England to the States many years earlier and although they were both living the American dream they never lost touch with their friends back home in Wakefield.

Sean met me first as was only fitting. He was there with me on the Golden Gate Bridge and he was with me on the Brooklyn Bridge and every mile in between. Thank you brother. I then ran and literally jumped into Stevie Walker's arms. "I knew you'd come!" I shouted. Steve Gage stepped up and gave me a great brotherly hug. I stepped back held my arms aloft and said "San Francisco to the Brooklyn Bridge... Get in!"

FB post 23 August 2013 Zoë Perrow
I'm so glad they were there to surprise you!!

We spent the next 30 minutes or so talking about how they had managed to keep everything from me. Walking up onto the bridge with Sean and the two Steves was a proud moment. We were four working-class lads from Wakefield, a town that no one ever heard about, and here we were talking about how we kicked America's arse!

FB Post 23 August 2013 Holly A Call
Awesome

We took plenty of pictures and then I was off again. I had seven miles or so to go until I got to Coney Island and the 'official' finish line. Normally this would take me just over an hour but as soon as I got off the Brooklyn Bridge I realised that all my energy had gone. I was shattered and it was, of course, bloody warm. Unlike the rest of the journey I had made no arrangements to meet up with Sean, in our excitement I had just told him to see me at Coney Island and this was a pretty dumb arrangement in the circumstances.

FB post 27 August 2013 Scott Bailey
I, probably as well as you and many others am still trying to get my head around what you have achieved! It's absolutely remarkable! You are absolutely remarkable!

Hot and emotional I was not moving well at all. The crowded streets seemed to go on forever. This time, thankfully, I had ten dollars in my pocket. I don't know how or why I had ten dollars, as I had not carried any money throughout the trip but I was able to buy some cold water and a chocolate bar to try and replenish my energy stores. It didn't work that well. The streets of Brooklyn were just as I imagined them. Tight, tall terraced housing on a grid system. Some areas appeared more affluent than others. It seemed a pretty cool place to live.

FB post 23 August 2013 Marsha J. Bowyer
So proud!

Rightly or wrongly McDonald's had been such a big part of the journey and it seemed only fitting that one of the final streets I ran down was McDonald's Avenue. This had not been planned in advance but I did chuckle a little. The road had a railway line running above it, which looked just like a scene from the movie *American Gangster*. It was typically New York – lots of noise! I have no idea how people live down there as the noise from the line was deafening and you could see people switch from talking to hand gestures every time a train went past. I found it a little strange and a little sad. After all the fantastic scenery America had laid out for me I was finishing amongst grime, litter and car exhaust fumes. I suppose it was pretty iconic of the area and for me, the city dweller, it was a place I could probably live in. It just wasn't what I had in my head for my last few miles of this magnificent run.

FB post 23 August 2015 Sarah Caton
Brilliant! Just brilliant!

FB post 23 August 2013 Sharon Falconer
Is this where you realise you left your keys back at the start & have to go back?

By this stage I only making walking pace, the emotion, my aching body and the heat of the day had taken its toll. Sean rang to ask me what was happening and how long would I be. I remember giving a short, sharp answer, "I will finish when I finish." I didn't want to fall out with people but I was on the last mile or so of my journey and, oddly enough, I didn't want it to end. I felt so much anxiety about the future. Things I had put off thinking about for so long: job prospects, finances, relationships... There were so many 'real world' problems that I had escaped from for the last four months and I was starting to realise they would still be waiting for me when I got home. I composed myself and made some phone calls.

Then, with one mile left to go my phone battery died. At the time I was devastated, my phone had been my constant companion. I almost cried but looking back now I know that it was probably the best thing that could have happened. I was on my own with my thoughts and could now think about finishing the run – no photographs, no phone calls, no video diaries – just me and the streets of Coney Island. *Mind you, the loss of the phone also meant the loss of Google Maps. Several wrong turns later I FINALLY saw the amusement park finishing point...*

Making my way up onto the promenade I had my first good look at the Atlantic Ocean. The sea was as blue as I had dreamt it would be and the bright white sandy beaches made me smile. I turned to my left to be greeted by my entourage. Deep down I had hoped for 10,000 cheering people, waving flags and slapping me on the back. I had five people waiting for me at the entrance to the beach. They were a small but important group. Sean, my ever, present brother, the two Steves and their friend and Laura Ku who I had met 100 days ago in San Francisco after the Bay to Breakers Race. How cool was it that she was in New York to see me finish? We hugged and had the all important ice cream before I walked across the warm sand towards the ocean.

For 100 days I had carried Jan's sobriety chip. I had carried Carey's for 94. Every morning and every night I took out the chips and held them in my hand before returning them to my pocket. The sound of them jangling together was the soundtrack to my run. As I approached the water I knew I had fulfilled their request. I reached into my pocket one last time. First, I took Jan's coin. He had managed to tie the whole run together. Carrying his chip from the day he met us in San Francisco to throwing it into the Atlantic Ocean for him was a huge honour. I doubt Jan will ever know how his chip and our meeting gave both Zoë and me faith that this journey would be a success. As I threw the chip into the ocean I was filled with pride. The journey was now complete for my friend Jan. His addiction was as far away from him as possible. Carey's story had also filled me full of hope, he was so happy to give up his hard-earned chip and showed immense faith that I would do as I had promised. Having someone show faith in your life is a fundamental part of recovery. Without someone's faith in your ability to stay sober the struggle ultimately seems pointless. Of course it is not, but we need someone to share our moments of success. I shared this moment with Carey as I threw his chip into the water. I believe in the power of the group. We stood united across America and we did what we thought was right.

Throwing myself in after the chips, I spent the next ten minutes diving and swimming in the ocean, cleansing myself of all I had been through. The water swallowed me up. It soothed my aching muscles and it felt good on my skin. My body began to cool down and I got a good feeling inside.

It was over, I had done it. I had run across the United States of America.

Keep the Faith.

FB Post 23 August 2013 Denise Taylor
What a truly inspirational achievement. That's some photo album you've got there. Very best wishes and huge congratulations to you. Now put your feet up for a while!

Twitter 3 September 2013 @Nicola_Rees
Amazing guest on the sofa tonight. Tom fitzsimons aka @ dryingout talking about his epic 3,000+ miles run across America! #run4sobriety

---

FB Post 3 September 2013
Tom has arrived at the BBC Leeds studios for tonight's interview – about 6.30

Tony Howell: That's one hell of a beard you're sporting there Tom!

Deborah Hough: OMG am thinking you have something living in it!!

Brent Nicholls: That beard is just plain magnificent!

Twitter January 2015 @DeanKarnazes
@dryingout An inspiring story, I wish you much continued success!

Stop-off points

Vallejo
VacaVille
Sacramento
Rancho Cordovo
Cameron Park
Placervile
Lake Tahoe
Carson City
Fallon
Middlegate
Austin
Eureka
Ely
Delta
Eureka
Heber City
Duchesne
Vernal
MayBell
Craig
Steamboat Springs
Waldon

Sleeping Elephant
Fort Collins
Greeley
Fort Morgan
Akron
St Francis
Atwood
Oberlin
Norton
Phillipsburg
Smith Center
Mankato
Belleville
Washington
St Joseph
Cameron
Chillicothe
Brookfield
Macon
Monroe City
Quincy
Meredosia

Jacksonville
Springfield
Decatur
Arthur
Rockville
Indianapolis
Springfield
Columbus OH
Zanesville
Wheeling
Washington
MT Pleasant
Somerset
Bedford
Fannetsburg
Paxtonia
Bethel
Hamburg
AllenTown
Newark

Coney Island

Total Days of Sobriety Pledged

3,667

(excludes lifetime: totals calculated daily)

Dedication Days

25 August	RIP Julian Charles, a friend who will be sadly missed.
19 August	Sponsor day – SRC Therapies.
17 August	Sponsor day – Signature Villas, Orlando Florida.
15 August	Sponsor day – Architecture 1B.
28 July	Today Tom is running for Jane and her children (from Australia).
24 July	A personal dedication from Tom for Charlie Engle who has achieved 21 years' sobriety. A particular quote of Charlie's that Tom draws inspiration from is 'Sobriety without Action is Pointless' and this led Tom to take action by setting up Run4Sobriety.
8 July	For Brian, Kerri, Sinead, Brian, & in memory of Fiona Guilfoyle. May the road ahead be full of peace & love. xo Tara
4 July	American Independence Day.
30 June	Scott Bailey celebrating his 3'year sobriety anniversary.
21 June	Tom and Sean's Mum, Eileen – a birthday dedication.
16 June	Happy Fathers Day – today's run is dedicated to all the 'Best Dads in the World' who on one day of the year are told what they already know... 'You are Awesome'.
15 June	Walter Hesketh, the original ultra-runner. 50 years ago he ran from Edinburgh to London in his slippers! RIP.
11 June	For everyone battling addiction and all the families and friends supporting them.

10 June	Annabelle Alice Lindley Born 7/06/13. Congratulations to all the family.
07 June	Steve Walker on celebrating becoming a US Citizen.
30 May	Holly A Call who celebrated her 1-year sobriety anniversary on 29th May.
28 May	Judy Woolfenden MBE RIP

Sponsors of RUN4Sobriety

Kenwood Travel – http://www.kenwoodtravel.co.uk/

Catlow – http://www.acatlow.com/

Rocktape – www.rocktape.net

Breaking the Cycles – breakingthecycles.com

SRC Therapies – Wakefield

Signature Villas Orlando – http://www.signaturevillasorlando.com/

Architecture 1B – http://www.architecture1b.com/

Shakoor Properties – http://www.shakoor.co

Lundbeck – http://www.lundbeck.com

About the Author

Tom was born in Belfast, Northern Ireland in 1974. Growing up with a love of football and life, Tom spent most of his time serving as an altar boy at his local church, St Bernard's, or at the 5th Belfast Cub Scouts, and would seldom be seen without a football at his feet.

Bright and ambitious, in 1986 Tom passed his 11+, which would have meant a grammar school education. Sadly this dream was short lived. The sectarian violence and conflict of the Northern Ireland's Troubles created a backdrop of unemployment and poverty that resulted in a family move to Wakefield, West Yorkshire. Tom, although scared of the future, embraced the move.

In new surroundings with his Irish accent attracting unwanted attention, despite making friends, Tom became shy and withdrawn and in 1988 after the sudden death of his father life began to unravel. Losing his ambition and energy, at the age of 13 Tom came to the conclusion that life was unfair.

The alcohol-fuelled years from 13 to 33 are punctuated with peaks of extreme violence and a desire for an early death. This young boy with a lust for life was spiritually and emotionally dead.

It took the love of one woman to save Tom's life. Zoë his partner showed a faith in Tom that awoke a giant. Her belief in Tom's abilities as a lover, father and as a man have allowed Tom to reach the outstanding levels you will read about in this book.

Tom still lives in Wakefield with Zoë and their two children Orla and Oliver. He also has two other sons, Mason and Niall, whom he loves dearly.

Having gained sobriety in 2007 Tom is now an international inspirational speaker who has shared his story with schools, businesses and sports teams across Europe. Tom also works as a personal trainer, coach and mentor to athletes and business leaders in the UK. Sharing his knowledge of health and fitness gained over seven years of his own personal transformation, Tom also devotes much of his time to supporting other addicts gain control over their lives.

Rediscovering his love of life, just like the young Belfast boy in the 1980s, Tom believes that the world IS a beautiful place.

To find out more about Tom and his work
visit: www.tomfitzsimons.co.uk
Follow Tom on Twitter @dryingout

Acknowledgements

Sponsors of Run4Sobriety

Without sponsorship adventure would be almost impossible. Getting to the start line of Run4Sobriety was made so much easier by the generosity of these great businesses. These guys had faith in the project and I am forever grateful for their kindness.

Kenwood Travel – www.kenwoodtravel.co.uk

Catlow – www.acatlow.com

Rocktape – www.rocktape.net

Breaking the Cycles – www.breakingthecycles.com

SRC Therapies – Wakefield

Signature Villas Orlando – www.signaturevillasorlando.com

Architecture 1B – www.architecture1b.com

Shakoor Properties – www.shakoor.co

Lundbeck – www.lundbeck.com

We also had lots of individual sponsors who gave their own hard earned cash to help fund the project. I can assure you that every single penny counted. I cannot thank you all enough.

Crowd funders

The book you have in your hand was made possible by the investment of 118 individuals who believed in my journey and my story. Their investment allowed me to tell my story to the world.

Thank you all.

Accommodation

A special thanks to the people who gave us a place to sleep: Tintic Goldminers' Inn, Eureka, Utah; Holiday Inn, Quincy, Illinois; Holiday Inn, Jackonsvillle, Illinois; The Crowne Plaza, Spingfield, Illinois; Marsha's Vineyard, Arthur, Illinois; Old Brick Inn, Chrisman, Illinois. Thank you, sleep is always better when it's free. Special thanks to Stevie Walker and Steve Gage for looking after us in New York at the Marriot Times Square – this gesture really was the cherry on top!

My Team

Thanks to Jamie Nelson for the wonderful t-shirt designs and the run4sobriety logo. Your work is a gift I appreciate.

To Connor and Catherine, your part must never be forgotten. You both added to this journey by being authentic. You both gave support to Sean and I when we needed it most.

Sean, my dearest brother, never forget that without you this journey would not have happened. I cannot think of anyone else that would have endured me for that length of time without killing me. You started the journey as my little brother but finished it as my friend. I love you.

Zoë, Mason, Niall, Orla and Oliver. My full-time team. Each of you gave so much and asked for nothing in return. You went about your business with no fuss or drama even during times of great pain. I will always be grateful for the part you all played in Team Run4Sobriety. Take a bow.

And finally, to everyone who took the time to follow my journey. To those who talked to me, sent me messages and simply cared about why I was running. Every thought, every word of support enabled me to finish what I started.

Tom